MW00387992

THE GIFT OF

gathering

BRE DOUCETTE

Rooms for Rent Blog

HARVEST HOUSE PUBLISHERS
EUGENE, OREGON

CONTENTS

—

spring

25

summer

71

fall

117

winter

163

—

LET'S GATHER
WITH GLAD HEARTS

*They broke bread in their homes and ate
together with glad and sincere hearts.*

ACTS 2:46

Something sacred happens when we gather around the table with people we love. Beauty permeates our souls and nurtures everyone as conversation flows, laughter ignites, and the desire to stay lingers long after the food has been eaten.

That's what the gift of gathering is to me. It's not about a perfectly set table, although I love that too! It's about coming together, filling our bellies, and spending time connecting with those around us, whether that means family, friends, a repeat guest, or a first-time visitor.

I remember our first dinner party as a newlywed couple. I was so excited to have some of our married friends over for what we called a Friends-Giving celebration. It was right in the middle of the holidays, and I wanted it to feel like an extra-special event, one that promised the joy and fellowship of the season so our friends wouldn't feel the burden of "yet another holiday obligation."

I created handmade invitations out of scrapbook paper and tiny ribbon embellishments, and I used a gold calligraphy pen to address each envelope. Never mind the fact that I didn't know how to write calligraphy, the special touch added elegance to the event.

Like most young couples, we didn't have much money, so I was bound and determined to host the best dinner party ever with the help of simple choices, the right attitude, and the most valuable resource for someone on a budget—creativity. I poured over magazines to get ideas and capture visuals that fed my imagination. Then I would scour dollar stores and thrift stores for pieces that suited the mood I wanted to present. I couldn't afford any of the tablecloths that fit my vision, so I went to Walmart and bought discounted sheer fabric by the yard. Just like the gold calligraphy pen, this material offered an affordable touch of sophistication.

The morning of the party, I woke up with great anticipation. I immediately started in on housecleaning, followed by some food prep, and then the part I couldn't wait for—setting the table. A task some of us probably thought of as a chore in childhood became my favorite activity. First, I draped a simple white curtain on the table and layered the sheer fabric on top. No hem, no problem. I knew the candlelight would illuminate the beauty and not the unfinished edges or any other flaws in the evening's presentation. (That might be the best tip ever, right?) Candlelight is like God's grace for your table. It covers human error and lets the heart of the gathering shine.

Next, I spread out the supplies I'd gathered over the previous weeks and began creating what is now called a tablescape. (Back then it was just a pretty table.) With a sweet understanding that I was starting a tradition for our family of two, I chose to include the glass candlesticks we received as a wedding present. Alongside those focal points, I placed dollar store votive candleholders filled with tiny gold rocks and tealight candles. I felt a sense of purpose and delight the entire time I was making the arrangement. The minute I became focused on the purpose of the gathering—to celebrate people we loved and a season we cherished—my initial nervousness turned to excitement. The details, thoughts, and efforts became all about that purpose.

The night was lovely. I saw how special our friends felt when they sat at the table I had prepared. Everyone enjoyed the meal. Still, the true gift of gathering was the sense of community. We were *together*. My husband and I would have missed out on all of this if we had given in to second thoughts about opening up our tiny apartment and squeezing around our hand-me-down table covered with a curtain. A passion was ignited in me. I knew that whether we had a lot or a little in the future, we would always be able to welcome guests to our table.

From humble beginnings my passion was born, and I'm so glad we're sharing this time together. I can't wait to show you season-influenced tablescapes for everything from casual gatherings to elegant parties. We'll look at how each element and every special touch serves up delight. My hope is that the photographed details, my stories, and the decor ideas will encourage gatherings of your own. I close each portion by highlighting a gift of gathering and offering a blessing that can be read aloud to your guests or can simply be for your spirit's refreshment as you prepare for them.

So many gifts—to give and to receive—come to light when you open your home and heart and welcome people to your table. So much gladness awaits.

~ Bre ~

BRE'S
TABLESCAPE BASICS

—

Your table is your foundation. Whether it's a picnic table, a card table in an apple orchard (that's in here!), a breakfast bar, or a farmhouse table like mine, it's the blank canvas that is ready for your creative touches to make every gathering unique. No two gatherings are ever the same; however, we will use basic elements to prepare tables for guests to feast on.

We'll look at linens, place settings, and centerpieces, alongside additional elements and techniques that add dimension and style, which is where the fun begins...well, the fun begins the minute you start planning. So let's go to that happy place.

Planning

Start with the information found on a typical event invitation. This is your research stage of planning. Figure out who you are inviting followed by the where, when, and why you're gathering. Is it a "just because" get-together or a celebration of a holiday, birthday, life event, etc.? This info helps you brainstorm and become excited about the plans.

Let me back up a second. I should first let you know that I'm a habitual procrastinator. I learned the hard way that planning is my friend and not some mean taskmaster. Planning will be your friend too. When the stress kicks in, and we're fretting over a missing plate or hollering orders to our family, we can refocus on why we're doing this and who we're doing this for. It's not about us. Sure, we're incorporating pieces we love, but ultimately we're creating a welcoming space for *them*. When we make it about something it's not, we put unnecessary pressure on ourselves and turn into an unhappy, harried host who no one feels welcomed by. I've been that person. And then I learned to give myself plenty of time to get ready and prepare for my gathering.

I'll never forget the very first time I was ready before our guests arrived. I kept checking the front window to see if anyone was approaching and then running back to my table to see if I had forgotten anything. Finally, my husband told me to sit and wait for our company to come. After a few minutes, I let out a deep sigh of relief and said, "So this is what being ready on time feels like?" We laughed because we both had comedic images in our minds of the days when I would run around the house desperately rounding up items for the place settings, wiping smudges off plates with a towel, tidying up (aka shoving miscellaneous items into drawers), or any number of actions I could have done hours or *days* before.

I hadn't appreciated the joyful benefits of planning until that day. I was a convert the moment I opened the door to the first guest and welcomed them with a sense of peace and a mind focused only on them. Not focused on last-minute details or on a false notion of perfection.

Once you know the who, where, when, and why, you can start imagining and planning the look and feel for your occasion. The three creative aspects of the planning puzzle are mood, inspiration, and color.

{simple planning timeline}

THREE DAYS BEFORE

—

- Plan out your meal.

- Do any deep cleaning that needs to be done.

- Purchase any pieces you might be wishing to incorporate on your table, such as new table linens or stemware.

TWO DAYS BEFORE

—

- Pull out the items you intend to use on your table. Plates, silverware, candlesticks, other tablescape elements. This is particularly important for any items you don't use daily.

ONE DAY BEFORE

—

- For a formal or more elaborate gathering, if you can, set the table in advance. By not waiting until the day of the gathering, you will have more time to focus on the food and any last-minute cleaning.

- Prepare any food that can be made the day before.

DAY OF

—

- Get any food prep out of the way first thing in the morning. That way when you begin to cook, you're not losing time dicing vegetables or slicing cheese.

- Do one more surface cleaning to catch anything that may have shown up after the earlier deep cleaning.

TWO HOURS BEFORE

—

- Make sure you're ready! There's nothing like being caught still in your sweats.

- Begin cooking. I try to time foods so they are done about 20 minutes after guests have arrived. This gives me time to catch up with guests and pour drinks.

TWENTY MINUTES BEFORE

—

- Light candles and turn on some music. There's nothing like creating an atmosphere that contributes to the overall feel of getting together.

- Relax. Say a prayer. Think about the gift of gathering.

MOOD

We can set the mood we want by how we set the table. Every basic element has a purpose, and every special touch adds to the ambiance and overall experience as well. A word or two might be enough to get your idea wheels turning. Don't overthink this. Just ask yourself how you want the gathering to feel. What mood would you love to evoke in your guests?

LIGHT | CASUAL | LIVELY | SERENE | JOYFUL

CHILDLIKE | HAPPY | COZY | LOW-KEY

INTIMATE | REFLECTIVE | ROMANTIC | GROWN-UP

FORMAL | FUN | WHIMSICAL | LAID-BACK

CELEBRATORY | FESTIVE | ELEGANT | PLAYFUL

I use the term "mood" a bit loosely. It's the vibe your table will inspire. All I know is that asking myself about the mood I want to create often leads me to the best ideas. For each gathering, I will share the mood.

INSPIRATION

When I'm creating a tablescape, I have some truths I'm working with. The decor will be up for only a brief time, and my canvas is only as big as the boundaries of the table, giving me a certain amount of space to let my creative mind run wild. These aren't limitations; they become our invitations to play within those time and space parameters. You really can't make mistakes, and a tablescape isn't forever. It's the offering of a moment, an experience for the people we love.

My ideas start blooming at this point because I know who is coming and why we're gathering. I know the mood I'm going for. Now I identify my inspiration for the particular tablescape so I stay on track. It can be easy to either get carried away with too many additions or get stuck on exactly what to add. Sticking to a theme and an inspired concept will help. Making a list of some key elements you want to incorporate is a great way to remember the look and feel you are going for.

Maybe you're inspired by an era, like the Art Deco of the Twenties or a home style like country cottage. Inspiration for a gathering might come from a trip you took to Italy or a dinner you had at a chic restaurant. Did an online or magazine photo of a table setting stick with you? Or maybe the view from your porch is all the inspiration you need? I love movies, so I will often have a clear freeze-frame image and mood of a scene I want to personalize in my tablescape's style, presentation, and colors. Sources of inspiration are endless. We're so lucky.

COLOR PALETTE

Motivated by the mood and inspiration, I then begin to dream in color. Often, I am taking cues and borrowing hues from nature because every season of the year presents its own shades of beauty. Wouldn't you say that taking design and decor suggestions from God's creation is a very good plan? And a very good reason why you and I might be compelled to send out those invites and celebrate the show creation is putting on.

It simplifies planning so much to choose colors to suit the mood you're going for and the spirit of the season. For example, in spring I'm going for light and cool tones. If it's fall, I want warm, rich colors. My best advice is to choose and stick with three colors for a pleasing and cohesive table decor. This could include one color in three different shades or three different colors repeated throughout the table. A practical example is when I use fresh flowers. I like to have the main flowers coordinate with other colors on the table, whether it's in the dishes or napkins I use. The thread of only three colors keeps things from looking too busy and will help you decide which plates, glasses, and other elements to use.

Tablescape Techniques and Elements

TABLESCAPE: An *artistic* arrangement of articles on a table.

Creating tablescapes for me is so much more than just having a grand design. It's about putting together the tiniest details that welcome our guests to a memorable experience.

As you and I look together at each tablescape and gathering, I will spotlight some of the techniques used and some of the specific elements I incorporated. It will be as if you and I are walking around the table and discussing ideas and sharing favorite seasonal inspirations as we go. While all of these techniques or elements are not pointed out in each design, almost all are represented!

We'll start with the three primary elements and expand from there. You will have so much fun when you start adding to the ways you create beautiful settings.

LINENS

Linens hold a special place in my heart. Soon after my husband and I got married, my mother gifted me my first set of cloth napkins. I imagine I gave her a slightly bewildered look. However, it didn't take me too long to discover how using cloth napkins, instead of paper, made our dining experience seem more special. They were the added touch that made everyday meals feel a bit more meaningful and substantial.

{bre's essentials}

—

Here are my absolute favorite go-to items. On their own, this decor dozen can be all you need. However, they are also easy to add to or mix with other tablescape treasures. With these on hand, you will create lovely tables for years to come.

White plates

Gray plates

Antique silverware

Linen napkins

Mercury glass votives

Vintage glasses

Cake stands

Woven chargers

Oatmeal linen tablecloth

Candlesticks

Wood cutting boards

Twine or ribbon
(to tie around napkins)

I like real linen. It has an elegant feel, but the natural look of the fabric keeps things relaxed. Typically, if I want my table to feel more dressed up, I will add a tablecloth, and if I want to create extra layers, I might place another tablecloth on top or include a plush table runner. (HomeGoods is my favorite place to score real linen tablecloths and napkins at a fraction of the price.)

CENTERPIECES

Creating a centerpiece is a great way to add interest to your table for your guests. I approach this a few different ways. If I create a centerpiece that can't easily be moved, then I make sure to set up a serving station where guests can fill their plates. You could also strategically place a centerpiece in a tray so it can easily be removed from the table to make room for food when it's time to eat.

The centerpiece provides a significant way to share your personal style and set the mood of the gathering. You can use candles, an artful display of a seasonal element, or your favorite flowers from the grocery store. You and I will soon be touring different styles of centerpiece for each type of gathering, so you'll have a great list of suggestions and inspiration for your own ideas.

LAYERS

Layers add depth to your table, which translates to warmth, coziness, and visual interest for your guests. Envision a comfy sofa loaded with fluffy throw pillows and a cozy fleece blanket draped across it. You want to dive right in, right? The same is true when we create layers on our table. Okay, you might not want people to dive into your garland, but you do want them to dive into the conversation, the fellowship, and the gift of gathering. Here are some ideas to get you thinking in layers:

Linens: A ruffled tablecloth layered over another tablecloth. A fluffy fur runner or cozy fleece blanket. Burlap coffee sacks add texture and layers. And sometimes a simple table runner on top of a rough-hewn table is all you need.

Place settings: This is the prime spot to create layers on your table. I always like to incorporate pieces that will help elevate each place setting on the table. Chargers stacked with plates and layered napkins create "presents" to greet guests one by one. Using bowls instead of salad plates, depending on the food that is being served, adds height. Using name cards and wrapping napkins with ribbons and ornaments all add layers to your place settings.

Centerpieces: An old barn board placed down the center of my table is loaded up with candles or pumpkins. Pieces of driftwood stacked down the center of the table. A tray or a cutting board can be under a centerpiece, giving the table layers while also making it easy to remove the centerpiece if needed. Cake stands with seasonal fruit arranged on top, and just simply layering some branches of greenery around your centerpiece add to the overall layer of the tablescape.

CASUAL

FORMAL

ELEGANT

PLACE SETTINGS

Place settings are intimate. It's the one thing on the table meant specifically for a guest to experience. I love to make my place settings feel as unique as the tablescape itself, offering the individual sitting there to feel personally welcomed. Here are common pieces that make up a place setting. You won't always use all of these:

chargers	stemware
plates	salad plates
silverware	bowls
napkins	mugs

It's meaningful to have a place set just for us. It tells us we're welcomed, invited, and wanted. It gives us a sense of security, knowing we belong. When we take the time to prepare a seat at the table, we tell our guests, *You were thought of, your arrival was greatly anticipated, and you are important to me.*

Tip: When putting place settings together, consider alternating the colors and sizes of the plates while keeping the mood in mind. I always have white plates on hand because food looks best on them and they're easy to mix in. Then I can add a salad plate or a bowl in a fun color or pattern for visual interest and added personality.

HEIGHT & SILHOUETTE

The overall height and silhouette of your table-scape has great impact on the impression and mood of the presentation. If you think of a cityscape or a landscape silhouette, you know how shapes and lines become beautiful art before your eyes. When designing, I think of ways I can add to and vary the height and depth for an engaging silhouette effect. I will use all sorts of objects and tricks to keep it interesting:

cake stands	a collection of vintage bottles
candlesticks	
vases	tree branches arranged in vases that reach for the ceiling
trays	
buckets	pillar candles
stacked books	

If you haven't viewed table decor this way, imagine a table set where everything is the same height or shape. It feels compact and clustered, right? Or even disjointed. Nothing visually stands out to draw you in. A good rule of thumb is to never add anything so high that your guests can't see over it. I've been known to break this rule every now and again, which usually ends up resulting in my husband removing the item from the dinner table mid-conversation.

TEXTURE

Nothing welcomes you into a gathering more than when you use texture on your table. My husband teases me when we go shopping because I'm constantly running up to him, handing him some random soft item, and telling him to feel it and appreciate it as I say,

"Isn't this amazing?" This is the response I have to the tactile wonders around us in nature, in fabrics, and in surfaces that are easy to take for granted in our home.

The same is true when it comes to incorporating texture on your table. Some things you want to reach out and touch because they are so inviting. Incorporating texture is a great way to include "using the senses" when creating a table. It instantly adds warmth that will welcome you in to any scene. We'll explore multiple ways to create texture during the journey through the seasonal gatherings.

NATURAL ELEMENTS

Just as adding nature to a room in your home makes it come alive, so does adding natural elements to your table as well. This can be incorporated in a multitude of ways, but I always look for some tiny bit of nature to add to my tables. Typically, I lean toward reflecting what is taking place in nature outside my window and follow its seasonal cues. In winter, I love bringing in branches that are bare of their leaves and fresh boughs of cedar and pine. In springtime, I look for anything with the tiniest pop of green or twig chargers that remind me of bird nests. In summer, I love adding fresh flowers or treasures I've collected from the beach, such as driftwood and rocks. And in fall, give me all the pumpkins and deep-colored flowers. Whether it's pieces used in your centerpiece or a special detail on each place setting, adding natural elements brings life to your table that everyone at your gathering will enjoy.

MIX & MATCH

My favorite, and I mean favorite, thing is to mix and match pieces. In fact, it's rare that I would use all the same pieces from the same set of dishes. Maybe it reflects my fondness for a relaxed, eclectic look. Using this term, even if just in our own heads, can give us permission to play with elements in fresh ways and prepare a table that has a relaxed mood even when it's a more formal presentation.

Your guests will love this.

My first instinct is to shake things up. I might use dinner plates from one set and a colored salad plate from a different set on top. Now, before you imagine me standing in front of shelves full of different plate sets in my basement, you're wrong. I can see my husband rolling his eyes at the mere thought of this reality. I have one fancy set, one everyday set, and then my favorite white plates! I stick to my favorite colors and have just enough to create whatever I can dream up. How about you? Do you have pieces you've collected over the years? You can mix and match them for a one-of-a-kind look that adds charm to your table.

ANTIQUES

I'm drawn to antiques not only for their beautiful details, but for the eras they represent. I love period films and series. When I first started watching *Downton Abbey*, I was inspired to search high and low, through every Goodwill store, yard sale, or estate sale for anything that was real silver. I was determined, as if it were my part-time job. I brought home my dusty, tarnished treasures feeling as though I'd won the lottery.

Blending old and new, clean and rustic, and incorporating antiques are great ways to bring a personal touch to your table. Just like when you

decorate your home or accessorize an outfit, you choose pieces that speak to you. When I'm scouring antique stores, I only buy pieces I absolutely love. Sure, the stores are filled to the brim, but selecting only a few pieces that stand out to you is a great way to reflect your personal style when setting the table. Maybe it's a color or a detail or a patina that you love.

Incorporating antiques is such a fun way to add interest to your meal and celebrate a time when gathering around elaborate tables was not something you hurried through, but something you made time for. The craftsmanship of bygone eras was exquisite, and the resulting objects are divinely pleasant to the touch and certainly to the eye. Your tablescape will be richer for the addition of antiques and the sense of history *and* story they bring to a display.

These are some of my favorite antiques I look for:

candlesticks	trays
gravy boats	teapots to use as possible vases
salt and pepper shakers	
stemware	tiny bowls to hold fruit
plates	serving cutlery
silverware	ice buckets

SPECIAL TOUCHES

Taking the time to add a special touch is one way to show your guests you're glad they came. For example, a personalized place setting will delight guests young and old. I know because I do this with my kids. Even though it's the same table they have sat at day after day, if there is a pretty object, a chocolate treat, or a note at their place, they're beaming.

The gesture can be as simple as handwritten menus presented at each plate, a personalized name card, an individual dessert they to look forward to after the meal, or just simply some embellishments tied around their napkin so it resembles a gift. It doesn't take much to add a special touch to each place setting.

Don't forget to feed and satisfy the senses when you're considering special touches. Think about the *ooh, ahh* factor of a strand of twinkle lights or the glow of a candlelit table. And it's not always about what you see that creates the experience. What you smell, taste, and touch will also shape memories and impressions. I love finding out what some of my guests treasure and then making that part of the gathering. A favorite scent, a beloved piece of silver, a delectable sweet treat, a single gardenia at each place setting.

What you and your guests hear can definitely support the mood you are aiming for. Put on some soft music in the background. Set the mood with some classics, such as Frank Sinatra or Michael Bublé, or chose a radio station from Pandora. My personal go-to stations to play while gathering are: *Dinner Party Radio, Hipster Cocktail Radio, Easy Listening Radio*, and, of course, *The Holiday Party Radio*.

DETAILS

I close with this because every element, every technique we just explored has their value in the details they bring to the gathering experience.

I find my joy in tiny details. When I'm planning an event, I always look for areas where I can add small somethings that will manifest the mood and gift of gathering in big ways. My best advice is to become a student of such details wherever you go. This also makes life one amazing adventure in observation and wonder.

When I'm dining in a restaurant, I'll notice their light fixtures. At a bookstore, I'll take a close look at the moldings in the building. When I'm at an outdoor market, I take note of how the crates are stacked to display their goods and the way they tie little hand-stamped tags on their accessories. I strongly believe I love creating tablescapes because it allows me the chance to focus on and then share details that create an experience for my guests.

Give yourself the joy of discovery by paying attention to the details in this book, in your home, and as you go about your day. You will be pleasantly surprised how ideas and interesting visual finds out in the world can inspire ideas for your next gathering. Challenge yourself to add one intentional detail to your next table.

My Hostess Gift to You

Remember to take a deep breath. Don't strive for perfection. Be sure to stay true to yourself. Your guests are coming to fellowship with *you*. The pretty table is just to enhance your experience. The details you tended to will be felt and appreciated. All you need to do now is savor your time together with a glad and sincere heart.

spring

The first glimpse of a spring sun rising in the sky and spring green emerging from the soil is a happily anticipated sight. With it we welcome new life! Our spirits are ready for renewal at this point in the calendar, aren't they? How perfect is it that Easter, a celebration of the power of resurrection, comes during this time of year? The landscape itself proclaims the blessing that comes after the old has passed—new blessings are faithfully brought forth. Our days are lighter, and our hearts eagerly embrace the promise of refreshment.

In New England, spring announces its arrival with spectacle after spectacle. It shows off in the bursting-with-life buds on tree branches and flowers popping up from the ground. In my opinion, it's the fragrance of lilacs that indicate spring's obvious arrival. Their perfume transports me back to my childhood and the point when I fell in love with this season.

As a little girl, I loved to crawl beneath the giant lilac bushes at my grandmother's house. I would lie there and take in their captivating scent, gaze at the pale purple blooms, and daydream. Every inch of my grandmother's home and yard encouraged curiosity and creativity. When I wasn't hiding beneath nature's enchanted awning, I was gathering its bouquets one after another. My grandmother would let my sisters and me pick any of the flowers we wanted, even if it meant she had to hoist us up for prized clusters that dangled just out of our reach.

When our small arms could carry no more, we would bring our treasured clippings into her house and fill as many vases and pitchers as we desired and however we fancied. We did our best impersonations of floral designers extraordinaire. That's the thing: Arrange. Rearrange. Admire. Repeat. Every surface, from bedroom nightstands to my grandmother's retro '70s kitchen table, displayed the rewards of our efforts. The fun and freedom made me giddy with happiness. I'd end the day curled up in a cozy chair, usually wearing dress up clothes and imagining the day when I would have my own home and my own garden and my own gathering table to decorate for my family.

That day is here!

It's no wonder I absolutely love creating gatherings in the spring. My husband jokes that if we never had people over, our house would never be clean. There is a teeny bit of truth to this. (Is that so wrong?) Our home might be tidy, but it might not ever get a thorough, classic "spring cleaning" if I weren't preparing spaces to share with others. There is nothing like inviting some friends over for a dinner party to get me motivated.

The moment sunlight and tulips are part of the picture, I don't want anything in my house that reflects winter. I crave light and airy. It becomes all about fresh blooms and pops of verdant green. The same is true when it comes to planning my table for a gathering. I retire heavier pieces and pull in cheery seasonal elements like potted herbs, and I choose linens and stemware that remind me of garden tea parties I had as a kid. Everything is more playful when life is in full spring.

After the long, dark winter months when it's easier to be a hermit than a hostess, this season opens up the window and lets in the breezes of inspiration. And every bird, bud, and bloom encourage us to honor beginnings, possibility, and new growth. I might not be lying under a lilac bush these days, but you can still find me looking for ways to gather beauty and to bring it in one bunch at a time—or maybe ten—to refresh the people I love.

Let's celebrate all that's new and budding in creation *and* in our lives this spring. Spring. Even the name makes us want to jump right in. Shall we leap in together?

FARMHOUSE
WEEKEND TRADITION

—

I can't talk about my heart for tablescapes and gatherings without sharing my family's favorite meal—Saturday morning breakfast! When my husband and I were young marrieds without kids, we lived in the city. Every Saturday morning we could head out in any direction and have our pick of divine breakfast spots. Starting off the weekend together became our tradition.

When we started our family, we traded our city dwelling for an 1846 country farmhouse. With two babies under the age of two, going out to breakfast was a fantasy, not a reality. So I began this tradition in our home. Fast-forward a few years, and now Saturday morning is something the whole family looks forward to. It's our chance to slow down, connect, and be refreshed together.

As you and I begin our journey, I pray you find hope and grace in knowing that it doesn't take much to make meals special. Trust me. You can put store-bought muffins on a cake stand, and suddenly they are meaningful. When you set a place around the table—or the breakfast bar—you invite others to nourishment that feeds more than appetites. It feeds souls.

{setting the tone}

MOOD

Home, family, tradition, love. Farmhouse casual with a side dish of comfort.

INSPIRATION

I am inspired by the charming bed-and-breakfasts I've stayed in that dot the countryside and
coast of New England. Inviting communal tables and simple touches of beauty begin the day right.

COLOR PALETTE

Simple and crisp whites and creams. Repeating colors in the food, flowers, and linens
is an easy and pleasing way to choose refreshing wake-up hues.

—

fresh blooms

pantry candlesticks

windowpane napkins

white plates

stoneware mugs

creamware
serving bowls

white enamel
silverware

FARMHOUSE WEEKEND TRADITION

PREPARATION

Make the morning of a breakfast gathering easier with a menu option prepared the night before. I've included the recipe for my first make-in-advance breakfast dish. Another helpful trick is to prepare your tablescape the night before too. Take ten minutes in the evening to set up the basics: juice glasses, silverware, plates, and a centerpiece of flowers or fruit. When you walk into the kitchen early the next day, you'll feel that bed-and-breakfast joy.

HEIGHT & SILHOUETTE

Even for our casual breakfast, I bring out my favorite cake stands and serving platters. Cake stands add height to the table, especially when piled high with scones or muffins on them, and they elevate what's being served, making it easier to see the array of options. Fresh blooms tucked into a recycled bottle give a different flair to a traditional vase and tend to be a bit taller too.

CENTERPIECE

I invite spring into my home decor whenever possible. My favorite centerpieces are created after a hunt through my yard with clippers in hand. I like a single flower or a heavenly bunch of blooms from different bushes to create a country bouquet. Even branches sprouting new leaves are up for grabs.

Tip: Breakfast is supposed to be easy, so don't fuss over table details. For this simple bouquet I headed out to my backyard and clipped one bloom from each tree. Don't have a backyard to escape to? Forget the flowers and use a bowl of fresh fruit as your centerpiece.

PLACE SETTINGS

Simple place settings are an unexpected touch for a casual meal and set this time apart from a weekday breakfast when a bagel on a napkin might be the scene. White plates are my go-to staple because they instantly make the food stand out and feel just a bit fancier, even if you're serving up just eggs and toast!

LINENS

I love light and airy in the springtime, so these sweet windowpane napkins and matching table runner are ideal. Their casual charm suits this easy-on-you and easy-on-the-eyes gathering. Cloth napkins will elevate any event, especially breakfast.

SPECIAL TOUCHES

When I'm making our traditional family breakfast, I use pieces that illuminate farmhouse living. Simple pitchers and recycled glass most definitely. And nothing says farm breakfast like my favorite cow creamer! The strongest traditions are centered on simplicity, family, and doable touches. It's amazing how strawberries become a decadent side dish when transferred from the store's plastic container to a creamware serving bowl. A lovely sight indeed.

Farm-Style Ham and Asparagus Strata

INGREDIENTS

1 lb. fresh asparagus, trimmed and
  cut into 1-inch pieces

6 English muffins (you will need 8 halves,
  with the remaining 4 halves torn into pieces)

1 cup ham, cubed and fully cooked

10 eggs

1¾ cups milk

1¼ cups cream

½ cup Gruyère cheese, shredded and divided

½ cup Asiago cheese, shredded and divided

3 T. mustard, stone-ground or pub-style

1 tsp. salt

¼ tsp. pepper

DIRECTIONS

NIGHT BEFORE . . .

◆ In a large pan, sauté the asparagus 2 to 3 minutes just until tender. Arrange
  eight English muffin halves in a greased 9 x 13-inch baking dish, cut side up.
  (It's okay if some edges lightly layer over other edges.) Sprinkle the cooked
  asparagus and diced ham over the English muffins.

◆ In a large bowl, whisk the eggs, milk, cream, ¼ cup of each of the cheeses
  (reserving the remaining ¼ cup of each for later), mustard, salt, and pepper.
  Pour over the top. Refrigerate, covered, overnight.

DAY OF . . .

◆ Preheat the oven to 375°. Remove the strata from the refrigerator while the
  oven heats. Add the pieces of torn English muffins to the top. Press them
  lightly into the egg mixture, but don't completely submerge them. Sprinkle on
  the remaining cheese.

◆ Bake, uncovered, 40 to 45 minutes or until a knife inserted in the center
  comes out clean.

◆ Let stand 5 minutes before cutting.

THE GIFT
OF GATHERING

Behold, I am doing a new thing;
now it springs forth, do you not perceive it?
ISAIAH 43:19 ESV

After her last bite of Saturday morning pancakes, my daughter, Dannika, predictably asks, "Can we have breakfast like this every morning?" I smile every time. The rush to get out the door during weekday mornings makes that pretty much impossible, yet I'm thrilled that both of my children appreciate and delight in the value and beauty of beginning a day gathered around a table with their family. This one modest meal helps to center us and our kids. It isn't about which breakfast foods are presented, though everyone has their favorites; the refreshment is in the ritual itself.

You might look at your crew and think, *My kids will never put their phones down long enough to enjoy a breakfast, let alone every week.* But give it a try. You'll be surprised how this will give new life to your home. The gifts of this tradition are for everyone. If the home front is you or you and a spouse, I hope you'll start this for yourself or you and a neighbor. Beginning a day with visual and edible pleasures will feed your body, mind, and spirit in lasting ways. Celebrate beginnings . . . of new traditions and mornings spent with people in your life.

{blessing}

—

Lord, as we gather together around the table more regularly, I pray You will strengthen our relationships. Give us refreshment through rituals that unite our hearts in fellowship, community, and the blessing of beginnings. Deepen our gratitude for all that is becoming vibrant and fragrant in our life. May we use times with family and with anyone You call to join our table to point out the gifts we see beginning to unfold in each other. Give us our daily bread, Lord, so we are strengthened and inspired to offer seasons of meaning to others. Amen.

ENCHANTING ORCHARD PICNIC

—

New England is famous for its splendid fall season. However, this girl is quite fond of spring's fabulous floral parade that winds about our landscape in full color. Delicate pastels. Sunny yellows. Heavenly blues. Every scene makes me stop to soak in all the brilliant shades that stir a sense of possibility. Thankfully, the rush of creativity also inspires other forms of expression. My canvas and yours can be a table decorated with spring's cheery offerings. Our masterpieces can be experiences that call everyone to rejoice in the earth's bounty.

Thank you, dear spring, for so many options. Perhaps my favorite setting can be found in apple orchards. Magical, rustic, and enchanting. Trees that look fresh out of a fairy tale are covered in tiny white blossoms that cling to branches briefly before covering the ground in a spring snow. In just the right moment, surrounded by all that blossom glory, one feels swept away to another time. Blending lilacs with formal elegance sets the scene for this casual outdoor picnic.

We're headed for another realm. Let's escape to the outdoors with friends on a warm spring day.

{setting the tone}

MOOD
Happy and light. A little bit fairy tale meets bygone era formal with a whimsical wink to playing dress up as a kid.

INSPIRATION
For this orchard gathering, I am inspired by scenes of English garden parties of long ago; when every detail mattered and even the butter knife was too important to leave behind.

COLOR PALETTE
With lilacs taking center stage, I coordinated the rest of my colors around this elegant purple hue. Soft grays and light blues with purple undertones play to a sort of monochromatic feel, and sprigs of lavender add the final touch.

———

TABLESCAPE ELEMENTS

windowpane
table linens

antique silver

twig chargers

soft blue plates

plaid napkins

ENCHANTING ORCHARD PICINIC

PREPARATION

For any outdoor gathering, bring pieces that serve multiple functions and can be transported with ease. Once emptied, stackable crates can create a drink station. Practical is the new beautiful.

HEIGHT & SILHOUETTE

The floral centerpiece provides a peak in the tablescape's silhouette. Pedestal trays provide additional serving spaces while lending more room and visual depth to the table's display. Depending on the height and size of the centerpiece, sometimes grouping items together helps visually to pull it all together.

CENTERPIECE

A simple white enamel farmhouse pitcher is all that's needed to corral handfuls of fresh-picked lilacs. I didn't want anything that would distract from the patterns already used on the table, and the clean white lines of the pitcher play off the solid white dinner plates. Lilac branches can have up to half a dozen blooms on one branch, providing a large arrangement that spreads out over the table.

PLACE SETTINGS

Color is part of the place setting plan for this gathering. The blue-gray plates on top of white dinner plates complement the soft hues of the table linens and fresh lilacs. The cool undertone of the smaller plates pairs well with the antique silverware. Repeating the same three colors throughout your table is a great way to keep the eye moving while also presenting a cohesive mood.

ANTIQUES

To add to the old-world feel, I included my antique salt and pepper shakers and formal silverware along with other silver pieces. The linens and the lilacs also add to the vintage feel.

LINENS

A simple oatmeal-colored hemstitch tablecloth is the perfect base for the ruffled white linen tablecloth placed at an angle across the table. To emphasize the feel of a formal outdoor picnic, I used a windowpane dish towel just for the top of the table to play off the smaller plaid napkins at each place setting.

NATURAL ELEMENTS

Nature is not just our background but also our finest decoration! This setting includes a fresh lilac centerpiece, twig chargers, and another pop of purple with the sprigs of lavender tied into napkins. When I don't want to go overboard with flowers, adding little bowls of fresh fruit that tie in with the color scheme are a great way to incorporate color and texture without things feeling too fussy. Even food choices can include natural elements. A lemon loaf sprinkled with lavender is as pretty as it is tasty.

Tip: Don't have time to make some yummy treats before you head out on your enchanted picnic? Hit up your local bakery and pick out a few premade items to bring with. My go-to choices are sweet breads, coffee cake, muffins, or scones.

Outdoor Drink Station

SKILL LEVEL:
simple

TIME:
5 to 10 minutes

TOOLS:
crates or baskets to stack

SUPPLIES:
decanter
different-sized pedestal trays
glasses
straws
garnishes
additional trays for serving

INSTRUCTIONS

1. First, make your base. For this drink station, I flipped my crates upside down and stacked them one on top of the other.

2. Place the top crate at a slight angle to allow a small serving space on the larger crate below. This is a great spot to place straws or a sweet treat to grab with your drink.

3. Add an antique silver tray to corral items. Other kinds of trays, framed mirrors, baskets, or even a pretty placemat can define smaller areas within a larger space.

4. Bring in a few elements to match the key pieces of your table. The antique silver tray carries over the antique silver on the main table. Smaller bouquets or single stems of flowers used in the centerpiece and place settings are a nice touch.

5. Keep glasses nearby for convenient pouring that allows a guest to refill their cup when desired.

Your guests will love this station. It's easy to put together for self-serve beverages, and it helps to visually define the border of the outdoor gathering space without interfering with the view of the chosen setting.

THE GIFT
OF GATHERING

{
He put a new song in my mouth,
a song of praise to our God.

PSALM 40:3 ESV
}

Spring inspires. Just like the animals in nature, we and the world around us wake up from a winter's slumber to all the wonders of a life refreshed.

New life is coming forth and making itself known. From baby lambs toddling in the fields to leaf shoots and colored buds appearing seemingly out of nowhere—this season is one huge celebration of being alive. You and I receive the enjoyable privilege of offering a unique experience to those we bring together during these months.

When you lose the walls, you gain a bigger perspective. This outdoor party provides so much more than an everyday social time. Your special touches and creation's healing beauty invite each person to the joys of breathing in fresh air, sharing in vibrant conversation, and recognizing the new possibilities and praises God is bringing forth in them.

{blessing}

—

Lord, may we celebrate all the life and beauty You call into being around us. Everywhere we look,
You invite us to experience Your majestic color palette and the promise of refreshment. From Your hand
we are given all we need to walk our path and to share the journey with others. Lead us to gather people
in fellowship that feeds the possibilities You place in each spirit, each heart. Lord, may we proclaim Your
wonder through praises and creative endeavors that not only draw us to others, but guide others to
embrace the many gifts of Your miraculous creation. Amen.

INDOOR GARDEN PARTY

—

It's taken me a few years to fully appreciate gardening, but now there is little I enjoy more than getting my hands in some potting soil once spring hits. The anticipation is great. Who doesn't want to get outside after months of being cooped up inside?

I experience so much refreshment during those first warm days in the sun. I fill my terra-cotta pots with flowers and herbs and spruce up our outdoors spaces sweeping off any remains of winter. I still have a lot to learn, but I've embraced gardening as my way to welcome the season. It has become a treasured part of my routine and lifestyle.

We might not all have gardens to play in, but we can all create an indoor garden with this naturally elegant tablescape. If you're concerned because you don't have a gathering "green thumb," pluck and toss that worry like a weed. Then do what I do: Practice self-grace (a lot of it!) and plan ahead to make way for beauty. You'll experience renewed confidence as you plant seeds of hospitality and love and watch for the loveliness of fellowship to grow and bloom.

{setting the tone}

MOOD
Down-to-earth elegance and a vibrant sense of celebration.

INSPIRATION
The spring greens are a welcome change of scenery. I wanted my table to
feel the same way and resemble the beautiful, growing, thriving world outside.

COLOR PALETTE
When bringing the garden theme inside, I played off colors you would see in nature. I wanted the herb-filled pots
to be the main focus, so I kept all the other pieces on the table neutral, with a subtle touch of elegance.

fancy linens

glass stemware

seed packet favors

s e e d

terra-cotta pots

herbs

fine china

CENTERPIECE

A collection of herb-filled pots offers an artful display and is a fresh take on a centerpiece compared to a floral arrangement. The herbs also keep the atmosphere playful. With a multidimensional silhouette, guests first see the impact of the whole and then enjoy noticing the beauty of each individual plant. It inspires conversation.

NATURAL ELEMENTS

Terra-cotta means "baked earth," and it provides the richness the name implies. These aged pots filled with herbs are bundled on a rustic farmhouse table to create a soothing visual anchor along with texture and tone. The dark soil in the pots extends its own invitation. You want to get outside and plant something.

HEIGHT & SILHOUETTE

Because spring inspires me in so many ways, I took design cues from the silhouette of lush life outside my back door. Varied heights create a natural landscape look, as do the different shades of green in the plants. The different-sized pots and plants are unique to look at, and when grouped, they create an organic centerpiece.

LINENS

Embroidered, monogrammed linen napkins add an elegant touch to the otherwise rustic table. They bring a sense of tradition to accompany the terra-cotta. When my centerpiece doesn't feel overly formal, I will often choose supporting pieces to bring that feel out subtly.

PLACE SETTINGS

Fine china with a platinum-silver band reflect the shimmer of elegance throughout the place settings. A formal silverware setting tells your guests just what kind of gathering it is. Don't be afraid to go all out when setting your table. Those extra details are the special touches that will make your guests feel important.

SPECIAL TOUCHES

Party favor seed packets are a great gift to send home with your guests. You can find various styles on Etsy or Amazon, or you can create home-made ones like I did. Tying a single ribbon around each seed packet gives them the look of a present and provides your guests with inspiration to start planting their own garden.

Tip: Using a free template, cardstock paper, and an at-home printer, a botanical printable becomes a seed packet favor. Once it's printed, follow the envelope template, press down a few folds, and add a dab of craft glue. These easy seed packets are formed to make a beautiful favor for each guest to take home.

Aged Terra-Cotta Pots

SKILL LEVEL:
moderate

TIME:
15 minutes plus drying time

SUPPLIES:
terra-cotta pots
lime wash
chip brush
paper towels

INSTRUCTIONS

1. Wipe down the terra-cotta pots to remove any dust.

2. Lightly dab your chip brush into the lime wash, wiping off any excess on the sides of the can.

3. Without applying too much pressure, lightly swipe your chip brush left and right on the terra-cotta pot, allowing just the ends of the chip brush to touch the surface of the pot. This ensures that not too much wash will be applied to your pot at once.

4. Use a paper towel to blot or rub in any area on the pot to achieve the desired look. This helps add to the aged look.

5. Continue steps 3 and 4 until you have reached the desired finish for your terra-cotta pot.

THE GIFT
OF GATHERING

{ *I will rejoice in doing them good and will assuredly*
plant them in this land with all my heart and soul. }

JEREMIAH 32:41

Planting a garden takes time and preparation, and so does planning
an elegant tablescape like this one. Most of us don't throw seeds on
the ground without a vision for what will grow, and we don't just plop
down any old plate at each place setting. Intention matters. It becomes
the spiritual centerpiece of our hearts, homes, and gatherings. And,
oh the joy when the dream is realized in the appearance of stalks and
stems, blossoms and berries, or guests and good times.

With each gathering you host, you are cultivating your skills and
learning to envision the coming joy. Sow the seeds of your intention
by choosing the special big and small pieces and tending to the details
that will bring your ideas to life. What develops is an inviting table to
grow your community and nurture your guests. For this gathering, let
the potted herbs remind you to season your conversations with encouragement. Let the soil remind you to stay grounded in your love. The
intentional time you spend with others will reap the reward of relationships that flourish and make everyday life beautiful.

{blessing}

—

Lord, let us gladly sow the seeds of encouragement and kindness in our time of fellowship. May we season our lives with Your love and stay grounded in Your goodness so we bloom in purpose and with joy. Thank You for the gift of spring and the daily evidence of Your power to resurrect life. We experience this power in Your mercy so we can share it through work, relationships, everyday conversations, and special gatherings. Today we celebrate the wonders You prepare and the hope You plant in our hearts. Grow us in Your light, Lord. Amen.

summer

Summer welcomes us to a more carefree perspective and way of living. It's a time when we can let rigid schedules fall to the wayside without apologies. Lazy afternoons spent in the hammock are totally acceptable, and ice cream for dinner is welcomed by all. A time when birds singing in the trees and lawn sprinklers sweeping the grass create a soundtrack to simple joys and activities. It's a season to indulge in backyard barbecues, summer breezes, and outdoor gatherings of any kind.

Whether we are rocking on our front porch with coffee in the morning or gathered around a fire at the end of the day, we tend to spend as many of our summer hours outside as we can. This longing comes naturally and encourages us to slow down and soak in every moment summer has to offer. My memories of childhood summers are intertwined with images of running barefoot through the grass and, of course, the beach. Thankfully, my entire family—then and now—has the same mind-set: Summer doesn't truly begin until we make our first trip to the coast.

As a kid I used to roll down my window as we got close to see who could smell the sea air first! Miles before our eyes met the waves crashing on the horizon, you could smell the ocean and anticipate what the day exploring those sandy beaches would hold. Breathing in the salty air, playing tag with the waves, exploring rocks in search of crabs, squishing our toes in the sand until it tickled—these were all favorite rituals after a busy school year. Isn't it funny how even when we are no longer in school, there's still a summer breeze easiness that takes over the brain? It isn't as though most grown-ups get the season off from jobs and normal responsibilities; yet the sunshine fills us with a sense of possibility that shouts *Summer is here! Slow down and unwind!*

One way I make this time count is to embrace a carefree style for my gatherings, whether they are simple get-togethers or fancier affairs. I prep our outdoor spaces so they are always ready for entertaining. This means that on any given day, I can quickly move a meal outside without extra fuss, energy, or any second thoughts. I keep trays nearby to carry things to our patio area. We personally have far more gatherings during the summer than any other season of year. I'm not sure if it's because we're following the seasonal cues to slow down and relax or because we're so elated that we don't have to reschedule outdoor events due to a snowstorm, a rainstorm, or temperatures that insist we scurry back inside.

As you'll see in the pages ahead, I like to embrace every blessing of summer by allowing nature to set the mood for my tables. You could say that nature is the first guest I invite to all my gatherings. You'll see creation's influence in nearly every aspect of my tablescapes. From fresh flowers in a centerpiece to pops of blue that remind me of the summer sky to beach rocks used as place cards. These treasures bring me so much joy that I go a bit nuts hunting for them, and I sometimes call on my family to go to great lengths to indulge this crazy passion. (Well, they say crazy and I say *endearing*. Stay tuned for more confessions about this.) I go the extra mile or sand dune because I love to incorporate these seasonal gifts in tablescapes.

I would bet you and I are kindred spirits who want life to be about what matters most, including how we express faith, share beauty, and engage with others. And we want to invite others to share time under the sun or stars, or among nature's best accessories. Whether you become more active or more laid-back when temperatures rise, the carefree spirit of summer welcomes all of us to shed restrictive layers formed by past seasons' schedules or fickle weather. It gives us permission to sit back and relax, and to celebrate the freedom, refreshment, and opportunities for connection the summer has to offer.

DESTINATION DATE—BEACH

—

For my kids, summer equals freedom. They dive headfirst into the fresh waters of an open schedule after a school year full of indoor routines. Speaking of diving, I'll plunge right into my confession. Summer is about my freedom too, because everywhere I turn I find natural elements I want to bring home...and often do. My family jokes that the minute I smell the sea air, I'm on high alert to seek and swipe pieces of driftwood off the shore. (See, that's endearing, right?) I'm instantly drawn in by the weathered patina of wood aged and polished by the sea and the story it tells. My husband has given up asking, "What will you ever do with that?" when I point out a body-sized piece I want loaded into our trunk. Now he just smiles, nods, and makes sure my treasure makes it home safely.

Let's begin this season surrounded by such treasures, including someone special. I created this tablescape at the beach to share with my hubby. Whether you're trying to spice up date night, do something different for girls' night out, or create an adventure for your kids, this casual destination gathering breaks up routine and invites everyone to delight in the freedoms summer delivers.

{setting the tone}

MOOD
This is a kick-off-your-shoes mood to put any guest at ease.

INSPIRATION
Every feature is inspired by the wild beauty and shapes designed and delivered by the sea.

COLOR PALETTE
The grays, blues, and tans of an ocean scene create a setting that is serene and inviting like a secluded beach.

—

glassware

driftwood

TABLESCAPE ELEMENTS

beach rocks

succulents

gray-and-white
striped linens

rope

PREPARATION

The day before a destination gathering, I create a checklist of everything I need and then set out each item to be packed in the car. It's no fun to arrive at your destination without silverware! Done that. I pack extra trash bags and a roll of paper towels too. You'll save the day and your sanity when you think through your setting, your guests' needs, and your after-gathering cleanup.

HEIGHT & SILHOUETTE

A rugged and beautiful silhouette is easily created with pieces of driftwood. First, I stack them and then place white candles of different sizes on top of the wood to add some height and symmetry.

PLACE SETTINGS

To keep the look crisp and casual, I use white plates as the base with the smaller taupe plates on top. This simple pattern adds visual interest without feeling overly formal. My favorite element is the nautical rope used to tie around the napkins and keep them in place while adding dimension to the place setting. Simple glasses and silverware complete this casual table setting.

LINENS

Ticking stripe, seersucker, pinstripes! All of these are part of the language of summer. I chose pinstripe cotton napkins for this casual gathering. Choosing the right table linens can help reinforce the style or season of the gathering you are having. They also help showcase other themed pieces, such as the nautical chunky rope used in place of napkin rings.

CENTERPIECE

Beach treasures are beautiful and make for enjoyable conversation pieces, so what could be better for the centerpiece? Sea-polished rocks and driftwood are my favorites. Once I have placed the candles on the wood, the rocks and sea glass fill in nicely around them. A finishing touch of two tiny succulents embellish this nature-made centerpiece.

NATURAL ELEMENTS

This gathering is all about natural elements and the beauty they offer your guests. Automatically you have texture, a varied and rugged silhouette, and an unforgettable table. The smooth rocks from the beach and the driftwood aged and shaped by the sea present lovely opposites from the same shore.

Tip: Even though succulents aren't typically found at the beach, they add a fun pop of color to the otherwise gray-and-white centerpiece. Plus, they last for hours without water, removing the need to pack extra vases and water that would be needed for fresh flowers.

Personalized Stone Place Cards

Using what nature has to offer is a great way to stay with the theme of your table and add a personal touch. Writing either the names of your guests or a quick sentiment on a rock found at the beach is a great way to add a personal touch to each place setting.

SKILL LEVEL:
easy

TIME:
15 minutes plus drying time

SUPPLIES:
stones, large and smooth enough to write on

metallic pens, black markers, or white paint pens (choose what will show on the stone)

pencil

INSTRUCTIONS

1. Using a pencil, I like to sketch out the name or sentiment first. (This ensures I have enough space and don't mess up when using the paint pen.)

2. Once my pencil sketch is complete, I trace over it with a white paint pen.

3. Allow to completely dry before transporting (20 to 30 minutes).

4. Set the stone on each place setting for guests to take home as a souvenir from the gathering.

If you want to have a message instead of a name, consider simple words of invitation or encouragement: "Welcome," "Glad You're Here," "Guest," "Celebrate," "Loved," "Blessed." Or consider writing a verse reference as a word of encouragement.

THE GIFT
OF GATHERING

Freely you have received; freely give.

MATTHEW 10:8

Am I the only one who wants to sip lemonade through a striped paper straw and read a good book from June through August? My favorite rhythm of summer might very well be nap, eat, repeat. LOL. However, while our personal rest is important, we don't want to miss our chance to welcome others to a gathering where they can rest and be themselves. Planning a casual gathering at a fun location will be worth the effort. Can't fit a table in your car? No problem. Grab your favorite blankets and dine picnic-style. Don't have a beach nearby? No worries. Head to a river, park, or place that gives you space to breathe. After all, this is a season of freedom, and I don't just mean the Fourth of July...though this gathering would be fabulous for that! So promise me you won't get caught up obsessing over perfection. Gather the way you want with the people you want and enjoy the carefree days of summer together.

{blessing}

—

God, thank You for Your creation and the freedom to seek and savor the gifts that come from You. How lucky we are that You warm us like the sun with Your love and bless us to share it. May we honor the simplest treasures of friendship, nature, food, landscapes, lazy afternoons, brilliant sunsets, and time spent together. Every place we join in fellowship is the perfect destination because You are with us in spirit and in the relationships that endure the waves of life and become magnificent because of them. Amen.

ALFRESCO EVENING

—

The easy, breezy feeling of summer can be carried over into how we entertain. If we are excited to gather and are relaxed when actually hosting, we tend to be more present to our guests. We see them as the entire *purpose* of the get-together rather than as stressful distractions while we're making our table and house picture-perfect. Ha. You've probably felt the difference in events you've attended. When the host is happy and available, you feel special and genuinely welcomed.

I created this backyard patio tablescape with that spirit in mind and heart. You'll like it start to finish and will be able to sit back and enjoy your company. Dining *alfresco* to my mind means "open air without a care." Maybe it's because you can't see the dishes piled up in your sink? Or maybe because time spent outdoors offers a festive party feel whether you have two or twenty guests. When the sun dips beneath the trees, creation inspires us to relax and unwind. And when the stars come out to greet us...ahhh. Enough said.

{setting the tone}

MOOD

I'm going for the outdoor café feel. The mood and setting are casual and stylish.

INSPIRATION

When a movie scene features an outdoor dinner party set in California, I swoon.
In the summer, we can all pretend we live in the Golden State.

COLOR PALETTE

I want my colors as relaxed as the environment I'm creating,
so I took my cues from the simple black-and-white windowpane tablecloth.

—

recycled
bottles

TABLESCAPE ELEMENTS

wooden plates

charcoal bowls

smoky stemware

black flatware

wildflowers

PREPARATION

A week or so before the event, gather bottles to use for the centerpiece. If sticky labels cause you trouble, never fear! This simple solution removes them with ease. Fill a sink or large bowl with hot water and then add ¼ cup baking soda and ¼ cup dish soap. (Stir to be sure the baking soda doesn't clump.) Submerge the emptied bottles, soak for 30 minutes, remove, rinse, and dry.

HEIGHT & SILHOUETTE

Using different jars or vases is a great way to add height and depth. Here I used a collection of reclaimed bottles of several sizes. This eclectic mix is unified in color tone and creates a lovely silhouette. It makes quite a first impression. I love using recycled pieces because they tell a story. Everything about this is relaxed and laid-back and doesn't take much time at all.

CENTERPIECE

The array of bottles unified by color creates our functional and stunning foundation. Then I add the refreshing beauty of the wildflowers to create the actual centerpiece. What feels more relaxed and effortless than an arrangement of blossoms from your yard? Or grab a few bunches from the grocery store. If you buy similar mixed bouquets, choose three stems that are your favorite, and repeat them throughout so the arrangement is unified.

SPECIAL TOUCHES

Patio string lights, strung overhead, create the intimate feel of a garden pergola, while the soft glow casts a feeling of wonder as it draws our gaze to the stars. Do you have a portable speaker? Along with the lights, food, and tablescape beauty, the special touch of background music makes the alfresco experience pure refreshment for all the senses.

TEXTURE

There are lots of different textures incorporated here: soft linen tablecloth, sleek amber glass bottles, stoneware bowls, and wooden plates. Each unique offering makes its contribution to the whole look, and the result is warm and engaging.

PLACE SETTINGS

The wood plates have a laid-back feel. They are natural and unpolished, and yet they offer color and texture to the entire table. To coordinate with the white in the tablecloth, I placed a white salad plate on top of the charger and then a charcoal stoneware bowl. Situating the white plate between the two darker pieces provides an appealing contrast.

LINENS

Charcoal linen napkins with a tiny white hemstitch complement the charcoal bowls and the smoky gray of the stemware. I chose darker napkins to contrast with the lighter linen tablecloth. This arrangement is striking and soothing, a look you wouldn't get with brightly colored linens.

Tip: You can never go wrong sticking with black and white tableware elements. Using them in glassware and cutlery adds an unexpected modern touch to this classic color combo.

Fig and Prosciutto Flatbread Pizza

We love making flatbread pizza in the summer. It's light, and fresh ingredients are a great way to have it as an appetizer or a main dish. You can make so many variations of pizza, but this fig and prosciutto is a crowd-pleaser every time. Even people who don't like goat cheese have exclaimed how it creates just the right balance and complements the other flavors on this anything-but-ordinary pizza. (The recipe is for one personal pizza. You can multiply the ingredients times your hungry guests.)

INGREDIENTS

Premade flatbread crust (I use naan from the deli section at the grocery store)

4 oz. prosciutto

3 T. pizza sauce

⅓ cup mozzarella cheese

4 to 6 fresh figs, sliced

2 oz. goat cheese

4 oz. arugula

Balsamic glaze

DIRECTIONS

1. Preheat the oven to 425° and then bake the pizza crust alone for 7 to 10 minutes. (This helps the middle of your pizza cook all the way.)

2. Dice the prosciutto and lightly sauté until crispy.

3. Remove the pizza crust from the oven. Top with the desired amount of pizza sauce and then add the mozzarella cheese. Add the prosciutto and fig slices, and then sprinkle with the goat cheese. Put the pizza back in the oven and bake for 10 to 12 minutes.

4. Remove from the oven, top with arugula, drizzle with the balsamic glaze, and serve!

THE GIFT
OF GATHERING

A generous person will prosper;
whoever refreshes others will be refreshed.

PROVERBS 11:25

Your guests will feel cared for and refreshed in this setting. And you will love the pure simplicity of this shared evening in the magic of dusk or sparkle of starlight. Don't stress about having special outdoor furniture to be able to dine alfresco. More than half of the pieces I use are from inside my house. Not only does it make the outside space cozy, but this choice also creates an opportunity for guests to feel included. At the end of the evening, I have them help me round up everything that needs to go back in. It's quite fun and adds to the camaraderie and connection.

Don't let space logistics or concerns about whether you have the "right" furniture steal the joy of having people over to your home. The backyard oasis you create will refresh spirits, hearts, and relationships because it's all about getting outside and getting real with those you gather with.

{blessing}

—

Lord, we thank You for an evening like this to gather. We are grateful for the joy of the outdoors and the opportunity to be with those who encourage and restore us. May we always be generous of spirit and serve one another, knowing we are passing along gifts that come from You alone. Life is an adventure. Help us to not worry about it being perfect. When it unfolds under Your gaze and in Your creation, the flaws and wonders become evidence of Your grace. Bless us so that our souls will be refreshed and our words of praise will be renewed. Amen.

SOPHISTICATED SUMMER AFFAIR

—

It's always a privilege to create a gathering for my friends that is as intimate as it is fancy. Not too long ago, my husband, Jesse, and I were coordinating a get-together with friends we hadn't seen in a while. As our communication unfolded and it was time to decide on a place to eat, I offered up our home instead of a restaurant. Why not? Going out can be fun, but dining in provides many gifts. There is time to connect and have heart-to-heart conversations and let loose with the laughter. When new and old friends desire to linger and savor the fellowship, nobody is rushing us through dessert, asking to clear our plates, or placing the bill on the table. (That's always a mood killer.)

This gathering has the luxurious feel of an upscale restaurant, but it's really a grand affair of the heart *and* home. With some planning, you and I are able to create a sanctuary to make people feel pampered and appreciated. So feel free to say, "Let's gather at my house" with confidence. All you will need is a bit of effort and attention to nourish guests inside and out. That's what happens when people are served with love.

{setting the tone}

MOOD

This gathering has a hushed sense of joy and indulgence.
It's a special present waiting to be opened.

INSPIRATION

Five-star restaurants and breathtaking images of intimate
spaces inspire this night of pampering and serving special people.

COLOR PALETTE

My favorite colors to decorate with in the summer are blue and white.
This combination is elevated to elegance with deep blues.

—

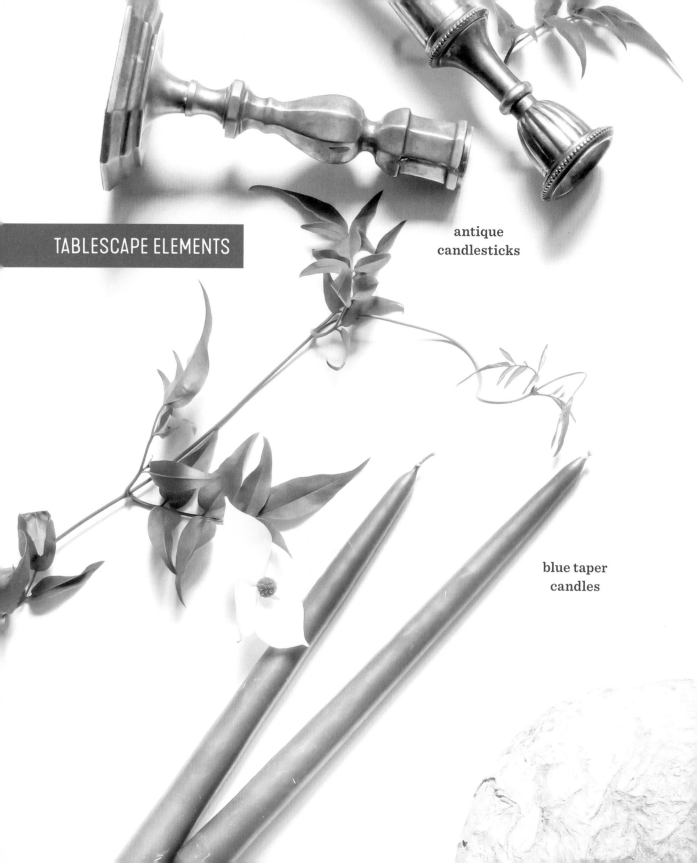

TABLESCAPE ELEMENTS

antique
candlesticks

blue taper
candles

white plates

blue linen
napkins

marble chargers

pewter silverware

SOPHISTICATED
SUMMER AFFAIR

MIX & MATCH

Delicate stemware and marble chargers are all about glamour, so I chose to balance them with the unpolished antique candlesticks and silverware. This way not everything is shiny smooth. Even for a fancy tablescape, I try to mix and match my pieces so the look is never over the top. My table ideas always start with the goal of making everyone comfortable and at ease.

CENTERPIECE

When I'm planning a more sophisticated gathering, a lot of details need to fall into place. Sometimes, to simplify and beautify my life, I will order flowers to showcase in the tablescape, especially if it's for a special occasion or celebration. An amazing centerpiece created by a local floral designer and friend is the striking focal point for this gathering. And I must say, when I brought this arrangement home and put it on the table, it was as delightful for me as for my guests later that evening. Plus, I was able to enjoy it for several days. (A hostess gift for myself!)

TEXTURE

The weathered wood table is a beautiful, textured backdrop for this stylish setting. Its rough patina contrasts with the smooth finish of the marble chargers and glass stemware. Antique candlesticks tarnished by age also add texture and ambience to the table.

SPECIAL TOUCHES

A single flower placed at each setting becomes a personal invitation to a beautiful time with friends. Attention to these last touches are often the efforts that let your guests know they were thought of and planned for, and that you're glad they are here.

LINENS

Grayish-blue linen napkins were used to coordinate with the overall color scheme. Because they are the only linens on the table, I wanted to tie the color of the blue glasses and the candlesticks together. Sophistication doesn't require a tablecloth when other elements are connected by color and a refined simplicity.

PLACE SETTINGS

White marble chargers are an elegant foundation for each place setting. I stack white plates and use blue linen napkins to break up all the white. The surprising oval shape of the salad plates creates a lovely effect.

Tip: Even though this table is designed for a more elegant affair, I serve a simple, down-home dessert to keep my guests feeling comfortable. Nothing says comfort like an old family recipe that tastes better when it's been made a day or two in advance.

Grandma's Rhubarb Cake

This decadent dessert is easy to make and will have your guests asking for more. This is one of my favorites from my grandmother's kitchen because it has an unexpected twist, and not just because it's a rhubarb *cake* and not a pie! It's light and fluffy and cake-like on top, while the bottom is divinely creamy, like a custard. I never reveal what type of cake this is until each guest has had their first bite, knowing they will be surprised...and ready for seconds.

———— **INGREDIENTS** ————

CAKE INGREDIENTS

1 (15.25 oz.) box yellow cake mix
  (be sure to include eggs and oil
  per cake mix instructions)

4 cups rhubarb, chopped

1 cup sugar

1 tsp. cinnamon

½ pint whipping cream

WHIPPED CREAM INGREDIENTS

¼ cup confectioners' sugar (or add to taste)

2 T. vanilla

1 pint heavy whipping cream

———— **DIRECTIONS** ————

1. Preheat the oven to 325°.

2. Prepare the cake mix batter per box instructions and then pour into a greased 9 x 13-inch pan. Chop the rhubarb and combine with sugar and cinnamon. Toss thoroughly, and then spread over cake batter. Drizzle ¼ pint whipping cream over the top and bake for 30 to 35 minutes or until a knife inserted comes out clean and the top is golden brown.

3. While the cake bakes, prepare the whipped cream. Place the sugar and vanilla into the mixing bowl and add the whipping cream. Beat with electric beaters just until the cream reaches stiff peaks.

4. Serve the cake with the homemade whipped cream. Delicious hot or cold.

THE GIFT
OF GATHERING

{

Whoever sows bountifully will also reap bountifully.

2 CORINTHIANS 9:6 ESV

}

Expending effort and paying attention are two personal investments that many in our fast-paced culture avoid in order to make life easier. But these two things deliver too many important gifts to be lost in the hustle and bustle of our busyness. An elegant dinner is not something you will likely do every night or even once a month. But let me encourage you to give it a try to experience something new and wonderful. The effort you put into an intimate gathering like this one is worth it. You are creating a sanctuary where you can connect with, serve, and nourish dear people.

   Not everyone will know how to communicate their appreciation, but you will be rewarded the minute you see the expressions on your guests' faces. When you and I open up our homes, we have the chance to serve as Jesus did; humbly and without fanfare. We can invite people to put aside the worries of the day and be fed. By the end of this evening, you and your guests will appreciate that a home sanctuary is not only made up of walls, a roof, and a pretty table, but is also formed in the tender connections between one another.

{blessing}

—

God, grant us the desire to pay attention to the lives and needs of those around us. Fix our hearts on serving and connecting. Give us the opportunity and desire to pour Your love into those we are blessed to call friend, family, or neighbor. May we be cheerful and humble servants who sow grace and watch for simple ways to be Your hands and to share Your gifts. Lord, we thank You for the sanctuary created by the connections made between those You bring together today and every day. We praise You for Your nourishment and peace that is ours in Your mercy. Amen.

fall

It starts with a spark. The tiny shimmer of a golden leaf here, a red leaf there. Evidence that time is moving forward, and the endless days of summer are giving way to cooler mornings and earlier sunsets. We jump back into the schedules and routines we so freely abandoned during the warmer months. Yet, as crisp air fills our lungs and radiant nature fills our view, we are reminded of fall's goodness. The familiar scent of pumpkin spice or warm apple cider on a chilly day is all the nostalgia I need to get into the spirit.

Here in New England, fall is a celebrated event. It starts at the end of August, and by the beginning of October our trees are bursting with dazzling colors. Leaf peepers come from all over to capture a glimpse or a photo of the splendor as the fall rainbow progresses from sunny yellow to fiery orange to brilliant ruby. As a kid, I had no clue how blessed I was to live in a region that experience's this magnificent transition year after year.

I've learned more recently that even though fall seems to come and go in the blink of an eye, and we are promoted to move on to all things Christmas, I long to take the time to embrace everything these months have to offer. Not to be swept up in the busyness of what's next, but to stop and soak in the here and now. I want to be more purposeful in creating or soaking in special moments, whether I'm apple picking with my family, taking a Sunday drive to gaze upon some fall foliage, or simply enjoying some of the season's soul-satisfying meals. As a girl, I might not have fully appreciated my good fortune to witness the emergence of fall's wonders, but as a woman, wife, and mom I don't take any of this for granted.

Maybe I'm able to shed summer and the scent of suntan lotion with sincere joy because I live in a small town that knows how to welcome a season right. The county fairs and a festive spirit pop up in late September and welcome us to indulge in comfort food, the bounty of the harvest, and, of course, the chance to gather. People are eager to come together in homestyle settings. And you know I don't need to be asked twice!

The moment I reach for a soft sweater, I am ready for nesting. With an ear-to-ear grin on my face, I seek out the warmer throws and fluff them up and drape them over chairs. It's the time of year when all I want to do is light a candle in my favorite fall scent and curl up with my favorite chunky, handknit blanket. Do you have a favorite blanket? If not, I encourage you to make that a goal this year. You'll want to be cozy while you plan your next gathering, because I strongly believe that after you nest, you're ready for a guest!

You can't help but feel grateful when you are surrounded by friends and loved ones and with a hearty meal on your plate. This *is* the season that offers up the Thanksgiving holiday. Though I think my heart would gravitate toward gratitude even if there weren't a national celebration to nudge me there. While I sip that pumpkin spice latte, I am most thankful to be intentional with the people in my life. I gladly let gratitude win over want or envy. I snuggle into a deep appreciation for the beauty and blessings around us...all from God.

Let's not let the season pass us by. Let's press in to stop and look around at God's beautiful masterpieces—not only the ones we see from our porch swings, but the ones we know as friend, spouse, child, mother, father, and neighbor. I hope these gatherings will be just the inspiration you need to join with others to celebrate the abundance of the harvest, express gratitude for dear relationships, and lift up praise for the Maker of it all.

FALL HARVEST GET-TOGETHER

—

The beautiful white-blossomed trees we enjoyed in the spring now produce an abundance of fresh, crisp apples. For me and my family, apple picking is our season opener. Nothing else will do. Have you ever spent a day in an orchard? It's pure heaven. The air is sweet and fresh and turns our cheeks as rosy as the fruit we pick. We spend the entire day outside harvesting our goodies and taking plenty of breaks to enjoy warm cider doughnuts and hot apple cider. It's a tradition my husband and I couldn't wait to introduce to our kids. They are just as excited as we are. Imagine that. Eagerness to work! With every bucket filled, the anticipation builds: *What delectable treat will be made with our harvest?*

I can think of no better way to kick off the season than by incorporating beautiful apples into a tablescape that will inspire us and our loved ones to celebrate the gifts of autumn. If you live in the city, head to your favorite weekend farmers market or grocery store produce section and start picking! In every setting and landscape, we can create this unique gathering experience and celebrate the harvest of blessings!

{setting the tone}

MOOD

*Fun. Refreshing. Laid-back and pure country. Right away, I knew I wanted
this gathering to feel as casual and comfortable as a flannel shirt.*

INSPIRATION

*Every element of this gathering is inspired by our family's joyful tradition and the many farm stands
we pass on our way home, which are surrounded by large, weathered apple crates.*

COLOR PALETTE

The palette prompt comes directly from nature. The deep apple-red pops against a neutral backdrop.

—

bucket of apples

TABLESCAPE ELEMENTS

freshly clipped
branches

copper flatware

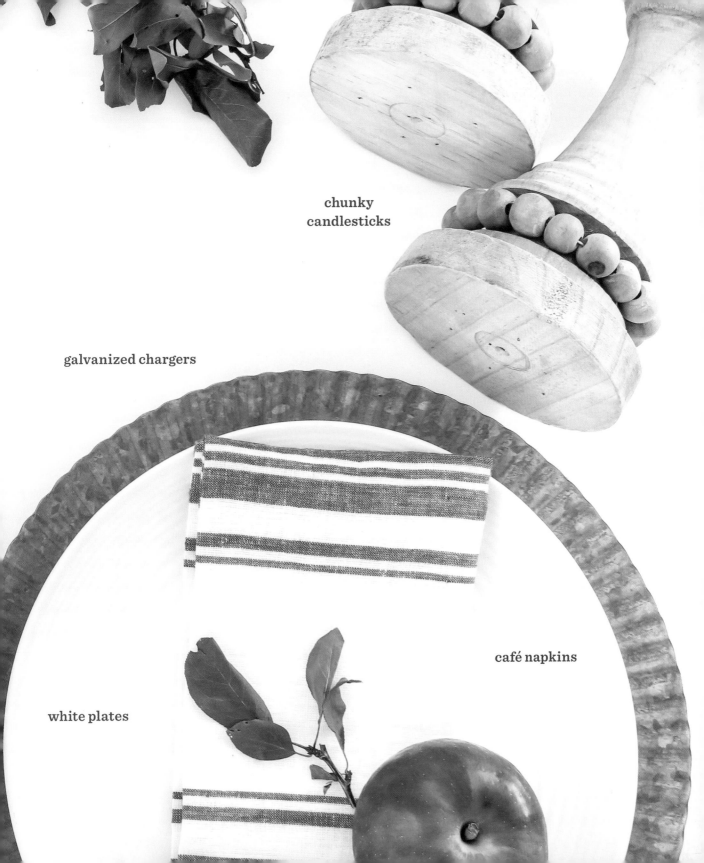

chunky
candlesticks

galvanized chargers

café napkins

white plates

HEIGHT & SILHOUETTE

Chunky wood candlesticks provide wonderful peaks and substance to this minimalistic table. They visually balance the bucket full of freshly picked apples placed in the center. The votives hanging from overhead tree branches add height to the gathering area because they pull your gaze upward, especially when lit at night.

CENTERPIECE

A bucket full of freshly picked apples grouped together with some chunky candlesticks keeps this table casual yet purposeful in evoking the mood and inspiration. The pop of red apples adds vibrant beauty. I gathered a burlap sack underneath these elements to add a foundation and nice layer to my sprawling centerpiece.

NATURAL ELEMENTS

Clipped branches woven around the centerpiece bucket add a carefree touch. This tablescape shines with seasonal elements to honor the harvest. You can achieve this look whether you are set up in a yard, on a patio, or at a neighborhood park. If you don't use apples, you can create a naturally lush centerpiece with tree branches and/or greenery from the floral department at your grocery store.

TEXTURE

Wonderful texture is everywhere here: the industrial factory-cart-turned-table, freshly picked fruit, leafy branches, and shiny glass layered on top of galvanized metal. And all this placed on top of the rough-hewn boards of reclaimed barn wood. The elements combine to present a warm and inviting first—and lasting—impression.

Tip: Wait until just before guests arrive to place the branches on your table. This will ensure they won't wilt too much before your gathering is over.

PLACE SETTINGS

Simple white plates stacked on galvanized metal chargers are the base for this place setting with shiny copper flatware that complements the tone of the warm apple cider placed at each plate. The galvanized metal chargers remind me of vintage apple pie plates commonly found in antique stores around New England. The café napkins with a red stripe bring all the elements together.

SPECIAL TOUCHES

The surprising use of a factory cart instead of a traditional table generates smiles and invites guests to pull up a comfy pillow instead of a chair. Just before this gathering, I placed cider beverages at each setting. When you have the drinks taken care of, you can greet each person as they arrive and direct them to their special place.

Tip: You might not be able to get your hands on an old factory cart, but a coffee table works just as well. Or stack crates and cover with a tablecloth. Perfect.

Spiced Apple Cider

Warm apple cider is found at most farm stands and apple orchards. It's a seasonal favorite in our household. This sweet/tart blend is mixed with warm spices. Once you take in the aroma while this drink simmers on your stove, you'll want to add this beverage to your own autumn traditions. There really isn't that much to it. Follow these simple steps, and you'll be sipping on a glass in no time. (And pouring your second.)

INGREDIENTS

CIDER

1 gallon good quality apple cider

4 T. lemon juice

¼ cup packed dark or light brown sugar, or to taste

¼ tsp. ground nutmeg

¼ tsp. ground cinnamon

¼ tsp. ground cloves

¼ tsp. ground allspice

SUGARED RIM

sugar

cinnamon

lemon wedge

cinnamon sticks

DIRECTIONS

1. In a large pot, add all of the cider ingredients and simmer on low 1 to 2 hours. Stir occasionally to ensure that the brown sugar has fully dissolved.

2. For the sugared rim, combine 3 parts granulated white sugar to 1 part cinnamon and place on a small plate. Use the lemon wedge to coat the rim of each mug and then press the rim into the mixture. Such a delicious and pretty addition to a harvest cup of cider.

3. Garnish with a cinnamon stick.

THE GIFT
OF GATHERING

{
*The L*ORD *will indeed give what is good,*
and our land will yield its harvest.
}

PSALM 85:12

Just as we harvest ripe fruit from the apple trees every fall, let's take some time to gather our friends and family and enjoy the harvest of fellowship. Friendships new and old blossom when we sow seeds of kindness. Together we can celebrate what is produced when we labor in love to help one another grow. This table honors creation, community, and all the blessings that come from God's hand.

You might not live near an apple orchard, but you do live near people you love. Don't worry about what you don't have; instead, focus on how to make a memorable experience. With special touches of beauty and attentive care, you will sow goodness into each person's life in practical and spiritual ways. Watch for the fruit to grow and ripen in your life and in theirs. And as often as you can, gather together to notice what God is doing so that every season becomes one to harvest what is holy and good.

{blessing}

—

Lord, we thank You for the bounty that comes from Your harvest. Whether we are fed from the abundance of freshly picked fruit or lasting gifts of beautiful friendship, we are nourished through Your goodness. I pray our hearts will reflect on all of Your blessings during this time. May we appreciate the breathtaking scenery that surrounds us and the inspiring friends who surround this table. Thank You for the gift of friendship, and I pray we would reap the dear and lasting benefits of fellowship. Thank You for the harvest, and the sweet reminder of the fruit that rises as we sow seeds of love into our friendships all year long. Amen.

FRIENDS-GIVING FESTIVITY

The shift toward cooler weather leads me to crave a gathering around the table and hunger for the opportunity to share a savory fall meal with friends. I want to soak in the joys of *this* season before the rush of the holidays hits.

In my opening chapter, I talk about our first "friends-giving" gathering. I highly recommend that you use this autumn tablescape as the perfect excuse to have your own friends-giving! Invite your favorite people over for a time of fellowship and express how thankful you are for them. If hosting a gathering of this size (or any size) has you feeling a little overwhelmed, opt for a potluck instead of taking on the task of making the entire meal. My husband never complains at the sight of more food showing up at the table. It's a great way to allow your friends to share their favorite seasonal dish. Even if you love to cook, it's nice to have occasions when you remove that pressure so you can focus on the people you are grateful to have in your life and in your home.

{setting the tone}

MOOD

Serene, intimate, and abundant. This is an adults "night in" dinner party that offers the treat of a formal yet cozy mood.

INSPIRATION

Even more inspiring than the seasonal elements is the longing to share a warm meal around the table.
My guests and I are ready for the comforts of nourishing food and friendship.

COLOR PALETTE

I love the softer side of fall. These muted autumnal colors are a little less traditional,
adding a unique feel to the overall table with nature's own refined touch.

———

cream plates

TABLESCAPE ELEMENTS

pewter flatware

amber glasses

seasonal
flowers

muted-colored
pumpkins

bistro napkins

PREPARATION

If you plan for a potluck, check in with each guest a few days before the event to ask what they are bringing. This way you know which gaps to fill—whether you need a few more appetizers, side dishes, or another dessert. And if a guest is unsure what to bring, you'll have categories to suggest.

LINENS

The addition of a linen table runner to this farmhouse table dresses things up slightly and adds to the overall layered look of the table. Layering napkins in between plates softens the place settings, while a more casual napkin is used to keep things from feeling too formal.

CENTERPIECE

Nothing says fall like visiting a pumpkin patch—so why not bring the pumpkin patch to your table? This artful display adds a playful vibe to an otherwise formal setting. Muted orange, cream, and white pumpkins are used for a unique twist on traditional fall colors. A splash of green is visible in the eucalyptus branches tucked around the pumpkins, and the floral arrangements in soft seasonal colors bring the look together.

MIX & MATCH

I brought balance to my table by incorporating a blend of pieces: traditional plates paired with vintage glasses, and pewter flatware alongside casual napkins help make sure my table doesn't feel too elegant. I want things to feel put together but not so over-the-top that my guests feel underdressed. Using galvanized metal containers instead of shiny glass vases helps my centerpiece to not take on a traditional look. Each piece was carefully chosen for a well-blended look.

Tip: Keeping things cozy, I didn't want to take away from the beautiful neutral centerpiece, so instead a fall-colored tablecloth is draped over an end chair to add some warmth and create an inviting seat for friends who come to dine.

PLACE SETTINGS

The cream plates topped with ramekins bring height to the table. This presentation also showcases the yummy treat at each setting. To add a casual flair, I layered a bistro napkin with the plates. The gray stripe in the napkin and the pewter flatware visually connect with the color of the galvanized metal containers.

TEXTURE

The roughhewn wood table, shiny galvanized metal containers, and smooth surface of the pumpkins parade a variety of texture. Even the hobnail amber glassware makes you want to reach out and touch it. Texture adds warmth to the visual and physical experience.

Maple Pumpkin Custard

Why not entice your guests by showing what they have to look forward to after the meal? A personal dessert serving at each place setting is visually stunning. Making a dessert with seasonal ingredients, like this maple pumpkin custard, is a wonderful way to celebrate the special tastes we enjoy most in the fall.

INGREDIENTS

¼ cup organic sugar (I used coconut sugar)

6 large egg yolks

1 tsp. vanilla extract

¼ tsp. cinnamon

⅛ tsp. ground nutmeg

⅛ tsp. salt

½ cup milk

1½ cups organic heavy cream

⅔ cup pumpkin puree (or you can use canned)

½ cup pure maple syrup

DIRECTIONS

1. Preheat the oven to 300°.

2. Whisk the sugar, egg yolks, vanilla, spices, and salt together in a large mixing bowl or the bowl of your stand mixer. Set aside.

3. In a medium-size saucepan, whisk together the milk, heavy cream, pumpkin puree, and maple syrup. Cook over medium-low heat, stirring occasionally, until the mixture is hot but not boiling (about 7 minutes). Slowly ladle a small amount into the sugar and yolk mixture, stirring constantly. (If you pour it all in at once, the yolks will cook. You don't want that to happen.) Once egg mixture and hot mixture are roughly the same temperature, you can add the rest a bit more quickly.

4. Pour ¼ inch of hot water into a large, shallow casserole dish. Divide the custard evenly among six custard cups and arrange the filled cups, evenly spaced, in the dish. Bake the custards, uncovered, on the center oven rack for 45 to 50 minutes. The centers may jiggle a bit but shouldn't be too fluid. Transfer the custard cups to a wire rack to cool.

5. When the custards reach room temperature, cover and refrigerate for at least 6 hours.

6. Garnish with whipped cream, cinnamon, and chopped pecans.

THE GIFT
OF GATHERING

I will give thanks to you, Lord, with all my heart;
I will tell of all your wonderful deeds.

PSALM 9:1

This rich tablescape allows you to show family and friends how much you truly care about them. I've mentioned before how the simple act of setting the table will make guests feel celebrated. Such gestures and invitations mean a great deal. So many people are either too busy or are too distanced from the tradition of preparing tables for meals in their daily life. When you host a friends-giving and invite everyone to be seated at your table, you are providing a place for their hearts to be warmed and their spirits filled. This is the gift of sharing life together.

No special occasion is needed, and even if no formal thanks are given that night, taking the time to host a dinner and open up your home instills in your friends the truth of how loved they are and your gratefulness to call them friend.

{blessing}

—

*God, I pray that as we gather around our tables this fall, our hearts would be filled with gratitude.
Remind us of all the treasures we are given as we partake in fellowship that feeds our souls. I pray our
time together overflows with laughter and joy, and that our hearts and our homes will be warmed with
gratitude for all You have blessed us with. Help us to share from the bounty of this season of the year
and of our lives. Give us eyes to see those in need of friendship. I pray for new relationships to flourish
and old relationships to grow deeper, and that we would know we have a friend in You.
Bless this time together and this table that connects us to one another. Amen.*

THANKSGIVING CELEBRATION

—

When anyone asked me as a kid what my favorite holiday was, my answer was always an enthusiastic, "Thanksgiving!" I knew they expected me to say Christmas, but even as a young girl, I held this occasion as special and sacred. It was about more than just the delicious turkey. It was the time when our entire family, including distant relatives, would gather. Dressed up. Happy. Together.

And yes, it's still my favorite. I suppose to some it can be seen as the day we spend hours slaving away in the kitchen to prepare for the main event, only to have it be over in a fraction of the time it took to prepare all that food. But I choose to look a little deeper. I view those hours spent selecting recipes, polishing silverware, and preparing thoughtful details as my offering to care for and nourish my family. Every bit of the process is a labor of love. This gathering is about all that love poured into the food that is served and the table that is set with a thankful heart.

My hope is that your family and mine will appreciate this celebration of our many blessings.

{setting the tone}

MOOD

*All the nostalgia of an elegant dinner remembered as a kid
who occasionally got to dine at the grown-ups table.*

INSPIRATION

*From my childhood love of Thanksgiving, this festive holiday table creation was born.
All my favorite elements are wrapped up in one grand tablescape.*

COLOR PALETTE

*Copper and rose gold accents are used to add warmth you would typically get from fall scenery.
Brought forth in shiny metals, these tones add sophistication to this elegant table.*

—

pumpkins
and squash

TABLESCAPE ELEMENTS

gold beaded
chargers

fine china

rose gold
flatware

antique brass
candlesticks

bay leaf garland

PREPARATION

For an elegant spread like this one, my preparation starts a week in advance when I plan out the menu and pull dishes out of storage. I wash my dishes and press my tablecloth a few days in advance and then set everything on my table the day before. Give yourself time for fine-tuning. You'll be surprised at just how enjoyable hosting an elaborate gathering can be.

HEIGHT & SILHOUETTE

Antique brass candlesticks of different sizes are placed alongside the winding bay leaf garland draped down the center. This eye-pleasing pairing adds height and dimension. To add volume and an elevated layer to the table, fluffy white linen napkins grace the top of each place setting.

CENTERPIECE

A roasting pan isn't only used for cooking a turkey on Thanksgiving! Here, I load one with pumpkins and a variety of squash to create a seasonal centerpiece that's visually rich and easy to move as well. Placing centerpiece items in a tray or pan allows you to make space for all those wonderful meal offerings when it's time.

LINENS

An oatmeal linen tablecloth is the foundation for this elegant table. This look reminds me of chic wedding receptions where their tablecloths sweep the floor. White linen napkins in gold napkin rings add to the refined look used in the linens throughout this table.

PLACE SETTINGS

The holidays give me the best excuse to pull out all the stops when it comes to creating each place setting. I retrieve my nicest dishware from storage. It's the china set I inherited from an aunt. When things are passed down from one family member to another, everything feels special and meaningful. Even if you don't have an heirloom set, make this season the time to start some of your own family traditions. I can't wait for the day when my daughter, or perhaps my granddaughter, will want to inherit some of my treasured pieces.

MIX & MATCH

Who says you can't mix metals? One of my favorite elements of this table is the mix of antique brass, rose gold, platinum, and warm copper tones. This blending creates a vintage feel. It's classy and elegant while also creating a somewhat relaxed approach compared to a traditional matching presentation.

Tip: Not sure how you feel about mixing metals? Try two or three to start with, and make sure you have enough of each to use throughout the table so the design feels balanced. You might just fall in love with this eclectic look.

Seasonal Harvest Centerpiece

This is a modern, stylish twist on the traditional cornucopia used at Thanksgiving. It's easy to create and becomes a visual celebration of God's bounty. You can also simply move it from the table when it's time to showcase the beautiful turkey as the centerpiece. Place it on a separate dessert table or buffet so everyone can enjoy its beauty throughout the day.

SKILL LEVEL
easy

TIME
10 minutes

SUPPLIES
roasting pan or rectangular tray
one large pumpkin
a variety of ornamental squash (can be found in your grocer's produce department)
4 to 5 mini pumpkins
Optional: 2 candlesticks

INSTRUCTIONS

1. Choose your tray. Or in my example, a roasting pan! It only felt natural since I would typically see this around Thanksgiving time, and I love the warmth the aged copper added to my table.

2. Place your largest pumpkin in the tray first. I suggest placing it slightly off to one side so there is more room on one side for the ornamental squash. As a general rule of thumb, you do not want your largest pumpkin to be more than half the size of your tray.

3. If incorporating candlesticks, now is the time to add these. One on each side of the largest pumpkin creates lovely symmetry.

4. Next, place your ornamental squash or next-size-down pumpkin in the tray.

5. Fill the remaining bare spots with mini pumpkins or smaller seasonal gourds. Pomegranates and pears also add a beautiful color to make a seasonal arrangement.

THE GIFT
OF GATHERING

*Enter his gates with thanksgiving and his courts
with praise; give thanks to him and praise his name.*

PSALM 100:4

Thanksgiving doesn't have to fall all on your plate...literally! I used to think I had to be the "hostess with the mostess" and do everything on my own. But I ended up frazzled and stressed, and I didn't enjoy the special day to the fullest. I started to place the food as the main event instead of the gratitude. Now, my family divides and conquers. A few weeks before the gathering, we decide who will bring a side dish, dessert, appetizers, and, of course, we can't forget the dinner rolls!

When we invite others to our table *and* to the experience of contributing in their own way, everyone feels a part of something substantial: a family, a circle of friends, a sharing of blessings. I might not have been able to communicate this when I was a girl, but it's what I understood and treasured. The thanksgiving and praise that flow from full hearts is our collective offering to the Lord, who brings us together. This is special and sacred—it's the gift of gathering.

{blessing}

—

Lord, we thank You for reminders to focus on all we are grateful for! I pray our hearts would be filled with praise as we bow our heads and give thanks for those gathered around this table and the abundance of Your provision. May this time together remind us to be content and generous with what we are given. Help us to be a blessing to all those we encounter. We gather hope right here, among loved ones, so that we can go on from this table to share the wonder of Your unfailing love and the good gifts You so generously pour out. We praise You, God, and thank You for all You have blessed us with this season and every season. Amen.

winter

I don't know about you, but I get giddy once the holiday ads start rolling on TV. The sense of excitement I had as a little girl on Christmas morning stirs in me once again. We'll overlook the fact that those ads usually start on October 1 and celebrate the joys that come with the winter season. For someone who loves all things home, it's all about the cozy factor...so here in the Northeast when the air turns crisp and the landscape glistens, I beam with anticipation for the first snowfall.

When I begin planning get-togethers for this quarter of the year, I think in terms of the grand finale at the end of a fireworks show. After all, our biggest hosting holidays are during this season. But I also look at the personal reasons we bring people together. We celebrate the birth of Jesus. We honor the transition from old to new as we prepare to mark the New Year holiday. There is anticipation for all it will lead to. There might be hesitation or great relief to leave the current year behind. No matter what we've been through, we can welcome the hope of new memories to come.

This is the time I become most sentimental about faith and family, and the traditions that connect me to both. So many traditions ring loud in my heart. The playing of classic carols and seasonal favorites from Bing Crosby and Frank Sinatra often sets in motion my longing for traditions. Instantly, childhood scenes play out in my memory like an old home video. My mom decorating our Christmas tree, my dad waking us up on Christmas morning with jingle bells, the smell of homemade gingerbread at my grandmother's house, and large family gatherings around the table.

I pause to soak in the joy...this is where my love for gathering around the table began.

Our entire family would come together for the grandest meal. The anticipation was great because it was the one season we talked about most! We looked forward to it, and the excitement of being together filled the room. My mother and grandmother had an assortment of crystal platters they would fill with finger foods and appetizers. Somehow, just seeing the spread on fancy dishes made the entire experience feel elaborate and holiday worthy. It was a celebration of family and the threads that connected generations.

Now, as an adult and planning the holidays for my own family, I reflect on the traditions I was introduced to as a child. Happily, I build the anticipation of all the season has to offer for my kids. My heart delights in the excitement on their faces and their chatter about the traditions they look forward to most. Whether it's watching the same Christmas movie my husband and I grew up viewing year after year, or simply making holiday cookies in the kitchen with me, they are soaking in the offerings of winter.

If I ever doubted whether my kids would handle traditions with care, those concerns melted away the Christmas my son was four and was helping decorate our house for the holidays. I was awakened from my decorating state of bliss when he suddenly and sternly said, "No, Mama!" I turned around to see his little face looking so serious as he pointed and said, "The bells get hung on this door." He promptly moved my jingle bells to the door they had graced the year before. I knew in that moment traditions were not at risk in this home.

I pray our time together in this season serves up treasures of winter—peace, joy, and hope. That you would carry these with you as you savor established traditions and create some new ones. We'll look at styles ranging from laid-back to fancy—so you can set your table with love and exchange the gift of each gathering with those you share your life with.

RUSTIC WINTER GATHERING

———

The holiday season is all the motivation I need to invite people over and then do it again! It's also a time of year when it's easy to become bogged down because I'm trying to do everything with a little magic thrown in...from making homemade gingerbread houses to tying ribbons on packages. The moment I read a Christmas sign that declares "Peace on Earth," I instantly let out a deep breath—and my stress with it—and then I inhale God's peace. It helps me prioritize. I realize that just by keeping the details simple, I can do what I love to do most— gather with others to share *that* peace.

Hanging on to seasonal stress is one tradition you and I can let go of. If the holidays have you overwhelmed with too much to do, you can still create a special time without the chaos. This informal tablescape is ideal for a Sunday brunch or a potluck with friends. As we walk through worry-free touches, you'll be craving a simple, rustic get-together in no time. (And maybe even whistling "Let There Be Peace on Earth" as you prepare.)

{setting the tone}

MOOD
A blend of modern and natural elements creates a fun and fresh table.
It's all about keeping things relaxed for a laid-back holiday or even a post-holiday get-together.

INSPIRATION
In my daydreams, I am nestled up in front of a roaring fire in a picturesque country lodge.
This table delivers that warmth and rustic beauty to our homes.

COLOR PALETTE
A plain and simple presentation of color surprisingly casts great charm, so I chose a hearty
yet basic black-and-white background with a tiny pop of green and a bit of sparkle.

TABLESCAPE ELEMENTS

brass
candlesticks

branches

mercury glass
ornaments

gold silverware

buffalo
check
tablecloth

tree-slab
chargers

votive
holders

RUSTIC WINTER GATHERING

CENTERPIECE

Who needs flowers for a table? Simple greens will add just the accent you need. Votive candleholders are used as vases for the hearty snips of winter greens and branches. These small greenery bouquets fill in the space around the antique brass candlesticks. Any seasonal offerings can be used. Bay leaf adds a wonderful fragrance to the table, and it's a nice twist from traditional pine or cedar branches you would typically see used in winter months. Petite vases or small jars can also work well.

HEIGHT & SILHOUETTE

Antique brass candlesticks of varying heights arranged along the table in a staggered style add engaging depth. There's a certain wildness to the look because the candlesticks resemble trees growing in the forest. Used in clusters, they provide tiny pockets of space to be filled with more (but not too many) seasonal touches.

NATURAL ELEMENTS

Branches and tree-slab chargers add charming seasonal touches. A simple walk through the woods during the winter will provide you with plenty of branch choices. If you are in a warmer climate or an urban one during winter, try finding some faux birch logs to spread across the table to bring in that woodsy feel.

TEXTURE

Mixing different textures is a great way to add warmth to your table. Here the blend of the soft plaid blanket with the hardwood chargers highlight the down-to-earth vibe. Visual texture becomes its own feast with the glass of the deep-green tumblers, the clusters of bay leaves, and pops of shimmery gold in candlesticks and silverware. The mix and match of casual and elegant enriches the textural delight.

Tip: Taper candles are a great staple to keep on hand. They add instant height, and, when lit, they add that soft candle glow that everyone is drawn into. Look for sets sold in boxes, which makes storing them easy.

PLACE SETTINGS

I love incorporating real wood chargers during the winter months. I pair them with crisp white plates for a unique contrast of rugged and contemporary. To keep things casual, I grouped my silverware and napkins together with a simple knotted ribbon tied around each setting.

LINENS

Instead of using a traditional tablecloth, I opted for a flannel throw blanket. I love how this one foundational element immediately creates a casual look and an inviting sense of comfort. Simple white napkins don't compete with the pattern of the buffalo check. These linens help maintain the overall aesthetic of the table.

Hearty Winter Soup

One winter's day I was uninspired about what to cook for our dinner guests. I prayed for an idea. God brought to mind a family favorite soup recipe. *Soup? For company?* I was skeptical, but as I prepared the meal and the aroma filled the kitchen, I felt God's peace. I served the humble offering to the delight of the couple who had been, of course, craving soup. Once again, I was reminded that "fancy" is *never* a requirement for hospitality.

— INGREDIENTS —

1 lb. kielbasa, fully cooked and cut into ¼-inch slices

3 large carrots, sliced

2 medium onions, chopped

2 T. olive oil

1 bunch kale, trimmed and torn

4 garlic cloves, minced

¼ tsp. pepper

¼ tsp. salt

2 bay leaves

1 (14.5 oz.) can diced tomatoes, undrained

1 (15 oz.) can garbanzo beans or chickpeas, rinsed and drained

1 (32 oz.) carton chicken broth

— DIRECTIONS —

1. In a Dutch oven over medium-low heat, cook the sausage, carrots, and onions in oil for 5 minutes or until the sausage is heated through, stirring occasionally. Add the kale, cover, and cook for 2 to 3 minutes or until the kale is wilted. Add the garlic and cook 1 minute longer.

2. Add the remaining ingredients. Bring to a boil. Reduce heat, cover, and simmer for 9 to 12 minutes. Discard the bay leaves. Serve with a crusty loaf of bread and an optional side salad.

THE GIFT
OF GATHERING

{ *Glory to God in the highest, and on earth peace among those with whom he is pleased.* }

LUKE 2:14 ESV

We can let our expectations take us for a sleigh ride down the wrong trail. Breathe out that stress for perfection and breathe in God's peace so you can celebrate this time of wonder with friends and family. Once you exchange the worry for the peace of the season, you'll discover you have what it takes, emotionally and practically, to create a welcoming space for all who come into your home. An inviting table expresses joy and serves peace in a tangible, meaningful way.

I'm reminded of one of my favorite contemporary Christmas songs by Sara Groves, "To Be with You," which references gathering around the table as we thank God for abundant blessings. The simple pleasure of coming together is enough. Sharing peace with friends, family, and neighbors is a gift that will echo in their lives long after they have waved goodbye with one hand while the other is holding tight to a goody bag of Christmas cookies.

{blessing}

—

Lord, may we gather around this table to savor and sink into the simple joys and pleasures of this season. Calm our busy natures. Let us seek You first, the Prince of Peace, to refresh and fill us so we can bring Your peace to others. Remind us to look for those who are weary or wanting so we can invite them into fellowship. And when we become hurried, help us remain gentle and generous of spirit. Thank You, God, for this time to be together. May we celebrate the gift of peace this season and become a comfort and light to those around us. Amen.

ELEGANT CHRISTMAS HOLIDAY

One of my favorite things to do in any season is go to a fancy restaurant for dinner. I feel special in an atmosphere created with attention to pretty details. If you ask my husband, he will tell you I love *any* excuse to dress up. It's true! And this girl also gets a little excited about any excuse to dress up my everyday table. Christmas gives me the best reason of all—to welcome my loved ones in the spirit of joy.

If your mental dictionary translates "fancy" as "pricey and per-fect," let me clear the air: This is not about perfection. Too much real life happens in this home! And I wouldn't want it any other way. This gathering is about paying attention to the details so that this special occasion will feel far from ordinary. This version of fancy is evident in simple, meaningful touches that will delight dinner guests from the minute they walk in and see the festive table.

If you've ever considered hosting a more stylish evening, I can think of no better time than the holiday season. Many celebratory elements are already evident—the soft lighting of the Christmas tree in the background, eye-pleasing baubles like glass ornaments, the scent of fresh winter greenery, such as cedar and bay leaf. Every detail of this gathering will warm the hearts of your guests and remind them they are loved as you celebrate the holiday season together.

{setting the tone}

MOOD

I add lots of details and glitz to set the mood meter to "wonder and awe." 'Tis the season, right?

INSPIRATION

As I child, I loved watching Christmas movies, especially the scenes where the families are gathered around holiday tables set with the glamour of other eras. Nostalgia and nesting inspire me most.

COLOR PALETTE

When I imagined this tablescape, images emerged of a soft, neutral palette with shiny focal points. A plan was born to pair nature's glory with holiday shimmer.

—

TABLESCAPE ELEMENTS

white plates

silver chargers

mercury
glass

boughs of
greenery

ornaments

HEIGHT & SILHOUETTE

I staggered the mercury glass trees down the center of the table, starting with the tallest tree in the center and then worked my way outward, so the shortest trees were on both ends. This symmetry is pleasing to the eye. The plate chargers and the greenery also add layers of different heights to the full tablescape.

CENTERPIECE

This Christmas table shines with mercury glass trees nestled in between branches of cedar, bay leaf, and seeded eucalyptus. I love recreating scenes from nature, and this centerpiece resembles the snow-covered trees around my house. Not only is this arrangement simple and stunning, the scent of this seasonal garland is heavenly.

SPECIAL TOUCHES

Each place setting is styled to resemble a Christmas present. Just like the packages underneath the tree, the napkins were adorned with shimmery champagne colored ribbon, a mini mercury glass ornament, and some sprigs of greenery. It's a simple touch, but one that tells each guest, "This is just for you!"

TEXTURE

Fresh greenery placed down the center of the table creates the natural foundation for this wintery scene. The organic textures of the garland and the weathered wood table create a striking contrast with the shiny and smooth glass trees.

PLACE SETTINGS

For this formal occasion, I layered crisp white plates on antiqued, champagne-colored chargers that play off of the mercury glass used on the table. I love to mix and match metals, so stemware etched in gold was used to bring balance to all the silver.

Tip: When incorporating antique silverware, don't worry about having enough sets that match. Pieces collected over time add a unique element, leaving each place setting to feel personal. Opt for pieces that have similar finishes.

LINENS

Working off the natural tones of the table, I chose stylish gray hemstitched linen napkins to add soft texture to the table. When incorporating silvers and grays, don't worry about matching them exactly—just make sure the undertones are the same. The difference between cool and warm undertones becomes much more noticeable when items are placed next to each other. By setting things up ahead of time, you'll be able to make the best choices.

Glass and Garland Centerpiece

When placed on top of greenery boughs, mercury glass trees give the illusion they're covered with snow. Fresh garlands and wreaths are my favorite way to bring the season's beauty inside.

SKILL LEVEL: moderate
TIME: 20 to 25 minutes
TOOLS: clippers

SUPPLIES:
mercury glass trees in different heights
sprigs of greenery in three different types (I used cedar, eucalyptus, and bay leaf)

── INSTRUCTIONS ──

1. Place the mercury glass trees in a row through the full length of the table's center. Start with the largest trees in the center and stagger down to the smallest trees at the ends.

2. Gather your greenery to place along the center line. Start with your flat greenery as the base. Fill in around the trees, tuck in your cedar branches to appear as though they weave around the mercury glass trees.

3. Next, layer your second widest branch selection atop the flat greenery. I used eucalyptus, with its wide spray of leaves, because its texture differs from that of the cedar. Place sparingly so pieces of the cedar are still visible.

4. Add your third and top layer of greenery. I used bay leaf branches that tend to fluff up more than the other two types that were used. For this layer, trim the stems shorter, tucking in the bay leaf randomly down the centerpiece.

5. Finally, tuck in any ends, hiding them under leaves or the mercury glass trees. Don't overdo the layers, as you want your centerpiece to feel full but not too heavy. When you're finished, you should be able to see all three different types of branches used.

THE GIFT
OF GATHERING

{
Splendor and majesty are before him;
strength and joy are in his dwelling place.

1 CHRONICLES 16:27
}

It doesn't matter how big your table is or how many chairs are at it; what matters is with whom you share it. Whether you have a large guest list or an intimate family dinner, taking the time to add some unique details will make the gathering feel special. Sometimes, just simply setting the table is all you need to make it feel formal. Don't stress over perfecting every little detail. Jesus didn't ask for perfection; he came into the world in a humble stable. His arrival wasn't about making a show, it was about becoming the Presence of light and love.

Remember to enjoy the moment and be present to each person. Set aside anything that didn't get done or didn't quite turn out as planned. What unfolds is just as it should be. You are with people you care about, and you are making memories together while celebrating this holy season. When it comes down to it, that *is* perfect, don't you think?

{blessing}

—

*We thank You, God, for the blessings of family and special friendships. Help us to remember that
the gift of the season is not the extra "stuff"—it's the presence of Your love in the world. May we take
time to express gratitude for one another and for You. Fill us with wonder. Guide us so we would
turn our burdens over to You and release our worries. Let us make space in our hearts for You and the
words You speak to us. And during this time of year, Lord, give us a spirit of hospitality to invite people
into our lives without hesitation and with the joy that comes from You. Amen.*

A REFLECTIVE
NEW YEAR'S SOIREE

—

I become more sentimental and reflective as the days of one year come to a close and the threshold of a new year is in sight. I think that's why, after the rush of the Christmas season, I crave an intimate get-together, one I can create at a slower pace. I want to pay more attention to detail to truly make it special for each guest.

The desire to hibernate can be considerable during the winter months, so a gathering at this time of year—whether on New Year's Eve or soon after—needs to be warm and inviting. This table does not disappoint. Your guests will respond to the serene atmosphere created by soft candlelight. People crave an evening of special touches and reverence, and I'm reminded of this by my kids' reaction when I bring out the fine china. They *ooh* and *ahh* because even at their tender ages, they appreciate beauty. My daughter immediately wants to be a part of the preparation. In fact, she helped set this table. Then, when it's time to dine (you don't just eat when you use china, you *dine*), the two of them run upstairs to put on their nicest clothes before rushing back down with pride and delight. They are breathless with hope and anticipation.

If *my* kids get this excited, it's a lesson for all of us who tend to a table's details: The heart responds to the lovely touches and the chance to be swept away by the moment. So bring your guests together for a spiritually refreshing way to celebrate another new year and all the hopeful new beginnings that come with it.

{setting the tone}

MOOD

Intimate and elegant. I want everyone who sits at this table to immediately feel relaxed and pampered.

INSPIRATION

The snowy landscape outside my window and the treasured silverware from my grandmother
make me want to share meaningful beauty with others. Each time I use this silver, I think of my
grandmother caring for this very set so she could share it with future generations. It's about hope.

COLOR PALETTE

Winters here in New England mean snow and more snow! Keeping the seasonal elements
in mind, an all-white palette was my go-to choice. It's so simple yet elegant, which is just
how it feels outside when the snow is falling from the night sky. It's captivating!

—

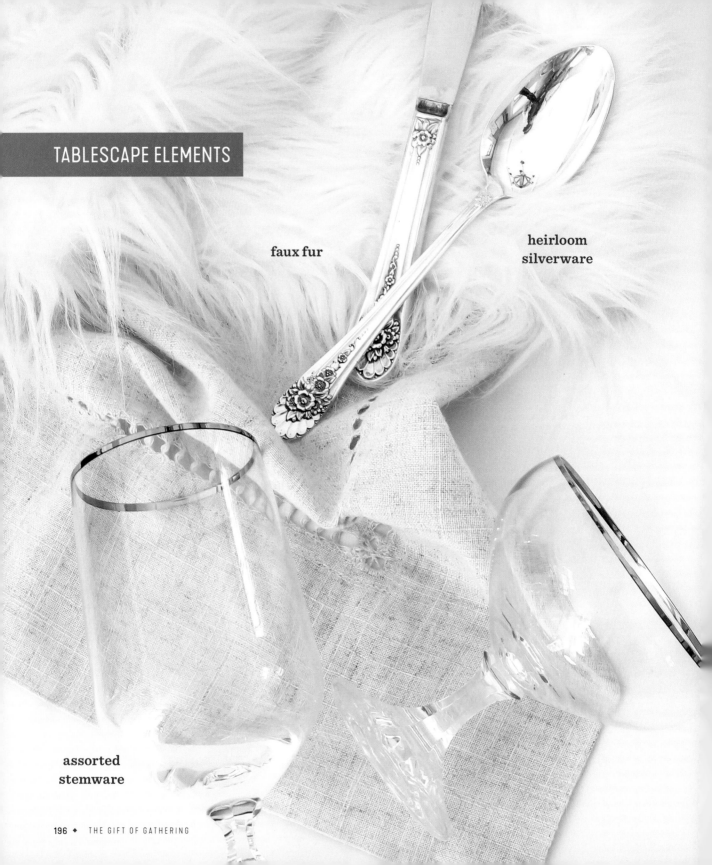

TABLESCAPE ELEMENTS

faux fur

heirloom
silverware

assorted
stemware

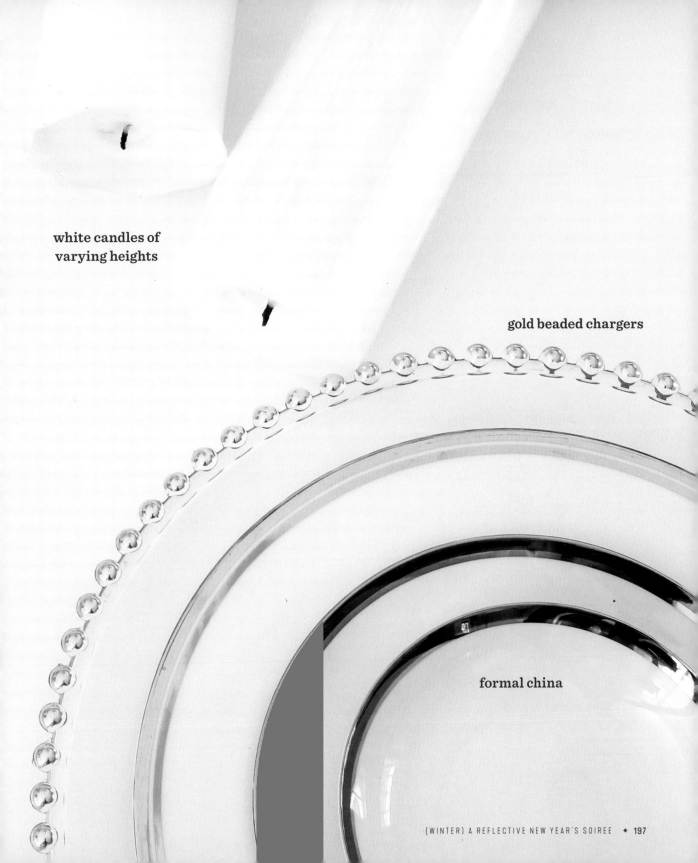

white candles of
varying heights

gold beaded chargers

formal china

PREPARATION

With a table this grand, I always start a few days before my dinner party. This gives me plenty of time to wash any linens or glassware that might have collected a little bit more than just dust while not being used. Setting the table a day or two ahead of time also frees you up to focus on the meal the day of and on the guests as they arrive.

HEIGHT & SILHOUETTE

Glass cylinder vases down the center of the table give the illusion of a longer table. Having them staggered helps keep the eyes moving, while candlelight reflecting off the glass illuminates the table and casts the perfect glow for this intimate dining experience.

CENTERPIECE

A shimmery centerpiece designed with glass and candles is breathtaking. From the glass cylinders to the stemware, down to the chargers, the overall effect is that of a crystal chandelier. It's magical. With varied heights of vases and slender pillar candles, the table comes to life. You know how no two snowflakes are alike? Well, let nature be your guide and plan to mix and match your glass candleholders. Use what you have or head to discount stores.

LINENS

A soft linen tablecloth creates a flawless foundation for the next layer: the faux-fur runner. This beautiful addition reminds guests of the fluffy blanket of snow outside the window. Elegant, simple, and rich. A winter scene unfolds before your eyes. To further this feel, I drape pretty white linen napkins from the center plate at each setting for a lovely cascading effect.

PLACE SETTINGS

I use all my finest pieces to serve up elegance. Delicate glass chargers with a gold bead detail are on the bottom, followed by china (inherited from my aunt), with a platinum silver band around the edge. To finish off this elegant and classic look, I use my grandmother's silverware. Seeing these items together gives me such a sense of connection to my family. Everyone who gathers at this table becomes a part of that.

SPECIAL TOUCHES

The extras that surround the table provide more opportunities for visual delights. I decorated the bar cart with a touch of greenery and a few pieces that add just the right amount of background shimmer. This cart can serve as a beverage, appetizer, or dessert tray. Or all three as the night's festivities progress.

Tip: A bar cart on wheels keeps hosting a breeze. It's easy to roll out of the way when more space is needed, or it can be kept at arm's reach, keeping those "extras" close by.

Festive Baked Brie

Successful gatherings are easier when you have go-to recipes that are also great crowd-pleasers. One of my favorites is this festive baked brie topped with red pepper jelly. It's a classic holiday treat with a fun twist. I pop this in the oven just before guests arrive so they're welcomed by the delicious aroma. I confess I make this brie only when I am hosting a party, otherwise I would eat the entire thing alone. In *one* sitting.

INGREDIENTS

1 (8 oz.) can refrigerated crescent dinner rolls

1 (8 oz.) round brie cheese

1 (10 oz.) jar red pepper jelly

1 egg, beaten

2 green apples, sliced

1 red apple, sliced

assorted crackers (for dipping!)

DIRECTIONS

1. Preheat the oven to 350°. Prepare a cookie sheet with nonstick cooking spray.

2. Unroll the crescent roll dough and separate into 2 sections. Press the dough firmly to form 2 squares, making sure to seal the perforations.

3. Place 1 dough square on the cookie sheet. Place the brie round in the center of the dough square. Spread heaping spoonfuls of red pepper jelly on top of cheese, equaling about ¾ cup. Then place the remaining half of the dough on top of the cheese round. Press the dough evenly around the side of the cheese. Brush the dough with the beaten egg.

4. Bake 20 to 30 minutes or until deep golden brown. Cool 10 minutes before serving. To serve, place the warm, pastry-wrapped cheese on a platter. Top with a few spoonfuls of the pepper jelly and arrange the apple slices and crackers around the cheese.

THE GIFT
OF GATHERING

*{ May the God of hope fill you with all joy and peace as
you trust in him, so that you may overflow with hope. }*

ROMANS 15:13

Even though the view out our windows might appear to be barren during the winter, this is a season of abundance. We all have so much to be grateful for, so many people to hug and love and remember. No matter what kind of year we've had, faith gives us an endless source of hope.

When this glimmer and glamour is all set up for a dinner party, my first instinct is to whisper a prayer for each person I have invited. Marking the beginning of a new year with others is incredibly special to me. God is unfolding plans and stirring hope for the days to come.

Once you try this elegant expression of celebration and hope, the captivating mood and memories might inspire you to start a tradition. And if your kids become as excited as my kids do, you won't save this tablescape to ring in the new year; you'll bring out your prettiest plates and glassware more often.

blessing

—

We praise You, God, that through every season of the year and of our lives, You are making all things NEW! In our times of celebration with loved ones, give us a heart that rejoices as we reflect on the special moments that have passed and anticipate the ones to come. Even through the dead of winter, You are planting new beginnings in our lives that will take root and grow in the future. Inspire us to watch for Your glorious works in the days ahead. As glass reflects candlelight, may we reflect Your hope and make a difference in the lives and world around us. Amen.

ABOUT THE AUTHOR

Bre Doucette is the author and creative voice behind *Rooms for Rent*, a blog with a signature and simple approach to design. She decorates with her heart and believes no matter whether you are a renter or owner of your home, or if you're an empty nester or a first-apartment dweller, everyone can "love the space they live in."

Along with writing her blog and being a wife and mom, Bre is passionate about creating beauty all around her in every aspect of life. Growing up in New England has shaped Bre's love for historic architecture, country settings, and coastal homes—all things that inspire her when she's creating spaces that are relaxed and comfortable with classic appeal.

Bre has been featured in various magazines, including *Better Homes & Gardens, Country Living, House Beautiful, Good Housekeeping, Yankee Magazine, Country Home,* and *Country Woman.* Her passion is not only to inspire women in their homes, but in their creative dreams as well. "Whether I'm decorating our home for my family or inspiring other women to love their spaces through my blog, I love serving others through the gifts God has given me. Wherever you are in your journey, I hope you feel inspired and encouraged to embrace the gifts that God has given you so you can bless those in your circles too!"

For more inspiration, connect with and follow Bre at:
www.roomsforrentblog.com
Instagram @roomsforrent

Farmhouse Weekend Tradition

1. Stoneware mugs— Farmhouse Pottery
2. Creamware serving bowls—Creative Co-Op
3. White enamel silverware—Birch Lane
4. Wooden pantry candlesticks—Farmhouse Pottery
5. White plates—Target
6. Window pane napkins and table runner—Target
7. Woven napkin rings—Farmhouse Pottery

NOT PICTURED

Vase—HomeGoods

Cow creamer—HomeGoods

Mason jar glasses—Marshalls

French press—Target

Cake stand —HomeGoods

Mug tree—Painted Fox Home

Enchanting Orchard Picnic

1. Cream pitcher—HomeGoods
2. Windowpane table linens—Target
3. Antique salt and pepper shaker—Family Heirloom (similar items can be found on Etsy)
4. Twig chargers—Painted Fox Home
5. White plates—Marshalls
6. Blue plates—IKEA
7. Antique silverware—Anthropologie
8. Plaid napkins—Farmhouse Pottery
9. Jelly mason jars—Target

NOT PICTURED

Cake stand—Painted Fox Home

Drink dispenser—Target

Picnic basket—Target

White pitcher—Ikea

Cutting board—PCB Home

White tablecloth—HomeGoods

Linen tablecloth—Wayfair

Crates—Local antique find
(similar ones found on Etsy)

Indoor Garden Party

1. Monogrammed linen napkins—EllaKate on Etsy

2. Simple stemware—Crate & Barrel

3. Terra-cotta pots—Michaels or Terrain

4. Seed packets—DIY

5. Fine china plates—Family heirloom
   (similar plates can be found at Crate & Barrel)

6. Ribbon—Etsy

NOT PICTURED

Antique silverware—Family heirloom
(similar styles can be found at Anthropologie or on Etsy)

Table—Restoration Hardware

Chairs—Restoration Hardware

Destination Date—Beach

1. Glassware—Crate & Barrel
2. White beaded plate—Target
3. Gray salad plate—World Market
4. Driftwood and beach rocks—sourced locally (similar items can be found in most craft stores)
5. Gray-and-white striped napkins—Target
6. Rope—Michaels

NOT PICTURED

Copper lantern—Target

Silverware—World Market

Table—Amazon

Succulents—Local Nursery

Candles—Christmas Tree Shop

Alfresco Evening

1. Amber bottles—Etsy
2. Windowpane tablecloth—Not PerfectLinen
3. Wooden plates—Crate & Barrel
4. White plates—Crate & Barrel
5. Charcoal bowls—H&M
6. Smokey stemware—CB2
7. Black flatware—Target
8. Napkins—TJMaxx

NOT PICTURED

Hanging lights—Amazon

Chairs—Painted Fox Home

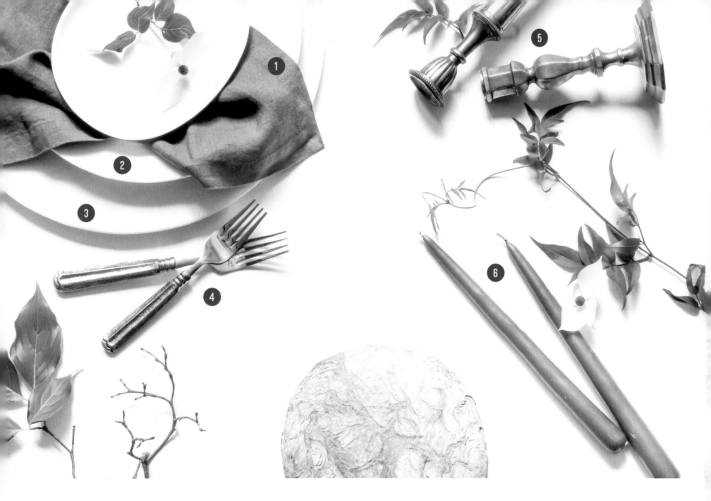

Sophisticated Summer Affair

1. Blue linen napkins—World Market
2. White plates—Crate & Barrel
3. Marble chargers—Caravan Home
4. Pewter silverware—World Market
5. Antique candlesticks—Found locally (similar ones can be found on Etsy)
6. Blue taper candlesticks—World Market

NOT PICTURED

Blue goblets—HomeGoods

Silver-rimmed glassware—Family heirloom
(similar styles can be found at Crate & Barrel)

Marble cutting board—HomeGoods

Vase—Painted Fox Home

Fall Harvest Get-Together

1. Apple bucket—HomeGoods
2. Copper flatware—All Modern
3. Chunky candlesticks—Pier 1
4. Galvanized chargers—Pier 1
5. White plates—Crate & Barrel
6. Cafe Napkins—William & Sonoma

NOT PICTURED

Glass mugs—William & Sonoma

Burlap—Michaels

Rolling cart—Local antique find
(similar ones can be found on Overstock)

Hanging votives—Michaels

Friends-Giving Festivity

1. Cream plates—Wayfair
2. Pewter flatware—World Market
3. Amber glassware—HomeGoods
4. Bistro napkins—William & Sonoma

NOT PICTURED

Cream bowls—World Market

Galvanized vases—Amazon

Table runner—HomeGoods

Plaid tablecloth—HomeGoods

Votives—Pier 1

Thanksgiving Celebration

1. Gold bead chargers—All Modern
2. Fine china plates—Family heirloom
   (similar styles can be found at Crate & Barrel)
3. Rose gold flatware—All Modern
4. Brass candlesticks—Etsy
5. Bay leaf garland—William & Sonoma
6. Silver-rimmed stemware— Family heirloom
   (similar styles can be found at Crate & Barrel)
7. Cream linen napkins—Wayfair
8. Gold napkin rings—Target

NOT PICTURED

Linen tablecloth—Wayfair

Copper votives—Wayfair

Roasting pan—Wayfair

Cutting boards—Painted Fox Home

Mixing bowl—All Modern

Rustic Winter Gathering

1. Brass candlesticks—Etsy
2. Mercury glass ornament—HomeGoods
3. Buffalo check tablecloth—HomeGoods
4. Tree slab chargers—Handmade
   (similar items can be found at Target or Michaels)
5. Striped ribbon—World Market
6. Votives—Pier 1
7. Gold silverware—Target

NOT PICTURED

Green glassware—Magnolia Hearth & Hand

White plates—HomeGoods

Paper ornaments—H&M

Galvanized urn—HomeGoods

Cloth napkins—Wayfair

Elegant Christmas Holiday

1. Silver chargers—Pier 1
2. White plates—Target
3. Mercury glass ornaments—HomeGoods
4. Mercury glass trees—HomeGoods
5. Antique silverware—Family heirloom
   (similar set found at Anthropologie)
6. White ornaments—Balsam Hill
7. Boughs of fresh greenery—Whole Foods or Trader
   Joe's during holiday season

NOT PICTURED

Tall stemware—Wayfair

Short stemware—Terrain

Silver napkins—TJMaxx

Velvet ribbon—Etsy

Reflective New Year's Soiree

1. Faux fur table runner—HomeGoods
2. Antique silverware—Family Heirloom
   (similar set found at Anthropologie)
3. Linen tablecloth—Wayfair
4. Assorted stemware—Family heirloom
   (similar styles can be found at Crate & Barrel)
5. White candles—Christmas Tree Shop
6. Gold bead chargers—All Modern
7. Fine china plates—Family heirloom
   (similar styles can be found at Crate & Barrel)

NOT PICTURED

Glass cylinders—HomeGoods

Beverage cart—Wayfair

Ice bucket—Local antique find
(similar ones can be found on Etsy)

White trees—HomeGoods

ACKNOWLEDGMENTS

First and foremost, thank you, Jesse, my husband and biggest supporter. You constantly encourage me to chase my dreams, and you never want any recognition for the support you give. To you and our children, Carter and Dannika, for allowing me to turn our home into my creative canvas no matter how messy the process may get. You inspire me and motivate me to make every tradition a cherished moment.

To Heather, for listening to that still, small voice that said I might like to someday write a book and encouraging me every step of the way! To Hope, for helping me realize I am just as much of a writer as I am a photographer, and helping me to eloquently put words to 12 different tablescapes so they would become a gift to all who read about them. To Harvest House, for seeing the potential in my work and giving me the chance to chase this God-sized dream and seeing my work in book form. And, of course, to the many hands that helped with the creative process to put all these photos and words together to create the finished book you hold in your hands.

To Mom and Dad. You were my first supporters and biggest encouragers to be who God created me to be. Thank you for making traditions matter and instilling them in me at such a young age. So much of what you shared has now become our family favorites.

And a huge thank you to all the friends and family who stood beside me and cheered me along as this book became a reality. Your encouragement and support means more than you will ever know!

Cover design by Nicole Dougherty
Interior design by Faceout Studio
Graphic on pages 25, 71, 117, 163 © T. Dallas / Shutterstock; Background textures on page 28 © rukxstockphoto / Shutterstock; page 39 © arigato / Shutterstock; pages 42, 56 © Jacob_09 / Shutterstock; page 74 © Golubovy / Shutterstock; page 88 © slava17 / Shutterstock; page 102 © Amguy / Shutterstock; pages 120, 134 © goldnetz / Shutterstock; page 148 © Boris Ryaposov / Shutterstock; page 166 © 35mmf2 / Shutterstock; page 180 © VolodymyrSanych / Shutterstock; page 194 © Moolkum / Shutterstock
All other photography by Bre Doucette
Floral arrangements by Christi Karjala
The definition of "tablescape" on page 17 is from www.yourdictionary.com/tablescape
All oven temperatures are in degrees Fahrenheit.

The Gift of Gathering

Published by Harvest House Publishers Eugene, Oregon 97408
www.harvesthousepublishers.com

ISBN 978-0-7369-7568-1 (Hardcover)
ISBN 978-0-7369-7569-8 (eBook)

Library of Congress Cataloging-in-Publication Data
Names: Doucette, Bre, author.
Title: The gift of gathering / Bre Doucette.
Description: Eugene, Oregon : Harvest House Publishers, [2019]
   not viewed.
Identifiers: LCCN 2018061373 (print) | LCCN 2019001915 (ebook) | ISBN
   9780736975698 (ebook) | ISBN 9780736975681 (hardcover)
Subjects: LCSH: Table setting and decoration. | Entertaining. |
   Seasonal cooking. | Holiday cooking. | Christian life. | Grace
   at meals.
Classification: LCC TX871 (ebook) | LCC TX871 .D68
   2019 (print) | DDC 642/.8--dc23
LC record available at https://lccn.loc.gov/201806137

Printed in China
19 20 21 22 23 24 25 26 27 / RDS-FO / 10 9 8 7 6 5 4 3 2 1